The New
Vegetarian
Cookbook

The New
Vegetarian
Cookbook

Heather Thomas

Foreword by Linda & Paul McCartney

LAUREL
GLEN

First published in the United States, 1998 by
Laurel Glen Publishing
5880 Oberlin Drive, Suite 400
San Diego, CA 92121-9653
1-800-284-3580

Library of Congress Cataloging-in-Publication Data

Thomas, Heather.
      The new vegetarian cookbook / Heather Thomas ; foreword by
Linda & Paul McCartney.
            p.   cm.
      Includes index.
      ISBN 1-57145-652-X
      1. Vegetarian cookery.   I. Title.
TX837.T464   1998   98-9979
641.5′636--dc21   CIP

Heather Thomas asserts the moral right to be identified as the author of
this work.

ISBN 1-57145-652-X

1 2 3 4 5 98 99 00 01 02

Printed and bound in Italy

Front cover: *Polenta with Sicilian Tomato Sauce, page 38 (top left);
Strawberry Zabaglione, page 120 (top right); Ravioli with Sage, page 30
(bottom left); Vegetable Couscous, page 40 (bottom right)*
Back cover: *Granary Loaves, page 130*
Page 1: *Dolmades, page 22*
Page 2: *Vegetable Couscous, page 40*

Contents

Foreword

By **Linda** and **Paul McCartney**

Cooking is one of the most sensual experiences—food has so many different textures, colors, aromas, and flavors—and to share that with family and friends is really satisfying. And cooking vegetarian food is even more rewarding. It's the healthiest, kindest, and most environmentally friendly thing that you can do for yourself, the animals, and the planet. What better place to demonstrate the benefits of a vegetarian lifestyle than in the kitchen—the more that people are offered delicious vegetarian meals, the more the cause will be advanced with every mouthful.

As Patrons of the Vegetarian Society in Great Britain, we're keen to get the message across to as many people as possible that the best food is that which doesn't hurt you or anything else. And so we're delighted to see *The New Vegetarian Cookbook*. The wonderful variety of recipes in the book demonstrates just how wide a choice of food nonmeat eaters have. The book has something for everyone who loves cooking and eating delicious, innovative vegetarian food—the recipes are fresh, healthy, and colorful, and designed to appeal to the busy cook who wants to serve attractively presented meals with the minimum of fuss and effort.

Vegetarian food is naturally healthy—it looks good, tastes good, and it's good for you. In fact, it's bursting with flavor and vitality. More and more people every day are embracing the vegetarian way of eating, and *The New Vegetarian Cookbook* will appeal both to newly converted and to more established, committed vegetarians. We hope you'll enjoy using this book and that it will remind you that being vegetarian is about living life, not ending it.

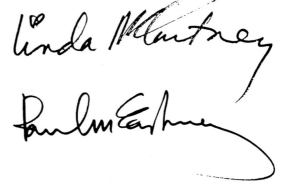

Foreword

by Heather Thomas

The *New Vegetarian Cookbook* invites you to discover the abundance of wonderful fresh ingredients available. It is full of delicious recipes, which are both nourishing and wholesome to the body and soul. The recipes reflect the infinite variety of vegetarian food, and explore international cuisines as well as some of our more traditional favorite dishes.

Bringing a vegetarian way of cooking into your kitchen need not be a formidable task, and the comprehensive range of dishes in this beautiful color cookbook will inspire you to extend your repertoire with considerable ease, whether you are a complete beginner or a more seasoned cook.

A vegetarian diet should never be thought of as one of denial, as cooking without meat can be refreshingly liberating. It really is an exciting and challenging cuisine. If you possess an appreciation for good food, whether vegetarian or not, you will fully enjoy this collection of contemporary recipes. Happy cooking!

Heather Mains.

Introduction

By eating vegetarian food, you can enjoy some delicious, sustaining dishes that respect animals and people, protect the environment, and provide a healthier, safer diet. You are also eating really healthy food that tastes good, looks good, and does you good.

An increasing number of people are now embracing vegetarianism and are adopting a meat-free diet as part of a healthier, and much more compassionate way of life, which does not involve the killing of animals or the abuse of the world's resources.

A well-balanced vegetarian diet provides all the nutrients your body needs for good health. Indeed, there is scientific evidence to indicate that vegetarians may be healthier than meat eaters. A vegetarian diet is typically low in saturated fat, is high in dietary fiber and complex carbohydrates, and high in protective vitamins and minerals. Medical studies have shown that vegetarians are less likely to suffer from such illnesses as heart disease, diet-related diabetes, cancer, obesity, and high blood pressure.

A vegetarian diet consists of the following:
- Grains
- Legumes
- Nuts
- Seeds
- Vegetables and fruit

It may be with or without the following:
- Dairy products (cheese, milk, yogurt, butter, cream)
- Eggs

It does not include fish, poultry,

meat, game, shellfish, crustaceans, or slaughter by-products, such as gelatin and animal fats. Yet vegetarian food is infinitely varied, interesting, delicious, and easy to cook and prepare.

Stumbling blocks

Most new converts to the vegetarian way of life are unaware of the hidden ingredients derived from the slaughter of animals in many everyday foods. For example, gelatin (made from animal ligaments, tendons, and bones) is often found in candy, ice cream and other dairy products. Animal fats (carcass fats) may be present in cookies, cakes, and some margarines.

Many types of cheese are made with rennet, a substance that is extracted from the stomach lining of slaughtered calves. However, vegetarian alternatives, made with rennet from a microbial source, are now widely available in most food markets and gourmet food stores. For more detailed information on vegetarian ingredients, turn to pages 10-14.

Nutrition

Just because vegetarians do not eat fish or meat, they can still get all the nutrients they need, i.e., protein, carbohydrates, fats, vitamins, and minerals, by eating a healthy, balanced diet.

Protein

Protein is essential for growth and repairing our bodies. Vegetarians can get their protein from the following foods:
- **Grains and cereals:** wheat, pot and pearl barley, rye, oatmeal, millet, maize (corn), and rice.
- **Nuts:** hazelnuts, Brazil nuts, almonds, cashews, sweet chestnuts,

Your healthy daily vegetarian diet

On a vegetarian diet, you should eat the following every day:

Grains, cereals, or potatoes	3-4 servings
Fruit and vegetables	4-5 servings
Legumes, nuts, and seeds	2-3 servings
Milk, cheese, egg, or soy products	2 servings
Vegetable oil and margarine or butter	small amount
Yeast extract fortified with vitamin B12	small amount

walnuts, peanuts, pine nuts, pecans, pistachios, and hickory nuts.

Seeds: sesame, pumpkin and sunflower seeds, sprouted seeds, and linseed.

Legumes: peas, beans, and lentils.

Dairy and soy products: milk, cheese, yogurt, and soy alternatives.

Free-range eggs

Proteins are made up of units called amino acids, and there are twenty in total. Although many of these can be made in our bodies by converting other amino acids, there are eight essential ones that can't be made and must be provided in our diet. Single plant foods don't contain all the amino acids we need in the right proportions, but we can get the correct amounts by mixing different plant foods. Indeed, as long as their diet is varied and well balanced, vegetarians need not worry.

Carbohydrates

Most carbohydrates are provided by plant foods, and they are our most important source of energy. There are three types:

Simple sugars: found in fruit, milk, and table sugar.

Complex carbohydrates: found in cereals and grains (bread, rice, pasta, oatmeal, barley, millet, buckwheat, and rye), and some root vegetables (potatoes and parsnips).

Dietary fiber: found in unrefined carbohydrates (whole-wheat bread, brown rice, whole grain cereals).

Fats and oils

You may be surprised to learn that we all need a little fat in our diet for good health. Fats can be saturated (hard animal fats, such as butter) or unsaturated (vegetable margarines and oils). A high intake of saturated fats has been linked to raised cholesterol levels and heart disease.

Vitamins

These organic substances are present only in tiny amounts in the food we eat. They are essential for good health and if you eat a varied diet based on fresh whole foods, you should obtain adequate amounts of the vitamins you need. The only exception is vitamin B12, which is not present in plant foods. However, most vegetarians can get as much as their bodies need from eating dairy products and free-range eggs. Here is a quick guide to vegetarian sources of vitamins:

Vitamin A: red, orange, and yellow vegetables (e.g., carrots), leafy green vegetables, peaches, apricots, eggs, milk, cheese.

Vitamin B: yeasts, whole cereals, nuts, legumes, seeds, green vegetables.

Vitamin C: fresh fruit, especially citrus fruits (oranges, lemons, limes, grapefruit), salad leaves, leafy green vegetables, bell peppers, tomatoes, potatoes.

Vitamin D: not found in plant foods but made in the body when the skin is exposed to sunlight. Found in milk, butter, cheese, yogurt.

Vitamin E: found in vegetable oils, whole grain cereals, eggs, soy beans, avocados.

Vitamin K: found in fresh vegetables and cereals.

Preventing loss of vitamins

1 Store vegetables either in the bottom of the refrigerator or in a cool, dark place.
2 Always prepare fruit and vegetables immediately before cooking them.
3 Don't add baking soda to the cooking water when boiling vegetables.
4 If possible, steam vegetables above boiling water to retain their vitamin content.

Minerals

Again, these are found only in minute quantities in our food, and they have different but very important functions in our bodies.

Calcium: for healthy bones and teeth. Found in dairy foods, leafy green vegetables, nuts, seeds, beans, and some dried fruit.

Iron: for healthy red blood cells. Found in leafy green vegetables, whole-wheat bread, molasses, lentils, dried fruit, legumes, eggs.

Zinc: plays a role in enzyme reactions and the healthy functioning of the immune system. Found in green vegetables, whole grain cereals, lentils, sesame and pumpkin seeds, cheese, and eggs.

Vegetarian ingredients

Food groups

You should try to eat some foods from each of these four groups every day.

Group 1
Cereals and grains
Provide: energy, fiber, B vitamins, calcium, iron
Examples: bread, pasta, rice, breakfast cereals

Group 2
Legumes, nuts, and seeds
Provide: protein, energy, fiber, calcium, iron, zinc
Examples: beans, garbanzo, nuts, sunflower and sesame seeds

Group 3
Fruit and vegetables
Provide: calcium, iron, folate, beta-carotene, vitamin C, fiber
Examples: fruit, broccoli, carrots, bell peppers, onions, potatoes, tomatoes, green leafy vegetables, salad, dried fruit

Group 4
Soy and dairy products
Provide: protein, energy, calcium, minerals, vitamins B12 and D
Examples: tofu, textured vegetable protein (TVP), soy milk, cow's milk, cheese, yogurt

Note: You also need small amounts of plant oils, margarine, or butter to provide energy, essential fatty acids and vitamins A, D, and E.

Here is a brief guide to some natural, healthy ingredients that you should try to include in your diet. Eat as many natural, unprocessed foods as possible and follow the easy guidelines in the box (left). Just make sure that you eat something from each of the four major food groups featured every day.

Beans

These are a good source of protein, vitamins, and minerals, and provide valuable fiber in our diet. They can be purchased dried or canned. When using dried beans, it is essential to soak them for several hours, preferably overnight, rinse them under cold running water, and then cook them in fresh water. Beans come in all colors and sizes— little Japanese aduki beans, black beans, black-eyed peas, speckled borlotti beans, pale green fava beans, lima beans, golden garbanzo, navy beans, pinto beans, red kidney beans, mung beans, and high-protein soy beans.

Beans can be added to soups and stews, tossed in salads, or dressed with a delicate creamy sauce or a robust tomato one. They are infinitely versatile and form the basis of many famous international dishes: Mexican frijoles (refried beans), black bean soup from the Caribbean, Jamaican rice 'n peas, and Boston baked beans.

Cereals and grains

Grains and cereals have been our staple food since ancient times, and are cultivated all over the world. They are most nutritious when the whole grains are used, as processing can reduce their vitamin and mineral content and eliminate the fiber. Thus it is better to eat whole-wheat bread rather than white bread, as the natural wheat germ and bran are removed from white wheat flour.

There are many different grains and it is a good idea to try and include as many whole grains as possible in your diet. You can choose

Alcohol

Vegetarians may be surprised to learn that they should take care when drinking or cooking with alcohol as many alcoholic drinks are fined (clarified) with animal ingredients. These include many bottled and canned beers. Wines may also have been fined with animal products, as is vintage port. Most spirits are acceptable with the possible exception of some whiskies and Spanish brandies.

from barley (pot barley and pearl barley), buckwheat (which is often cooked like rice or made into flour), maize, or corn (the ground flour is made into tortillas and polenta), millet, oatmeal (used in muesli, porridge, and desserts), rye (as in dark rye bread), and wheat (white and whole-wheat flours, cracked wheat, and durum wheat as in pasta).

Cheese

Cheese is a complete protein as it contains the eight essential amino acids that the body can't make itself. Rich in vitamins A, B, and D, calcium, and phosphorus, it is a very valuable food, although full-fat cheese is a major source of saturated fat, which can lead to raised serum cholesterol levels. However, many cheeses are produced using animal rennet, an enzyme obtained from the stomachs of newly killed calves, and these are not suitable for vegetarians. But vegetarian alternatives are available, produced using microbial or fungus enzymes, and you can now buy vegetarian versions of many of your favorite cheeses. When shopping for cheese, be sure to read the labels carefully on the packaging. Vegetarian cheeses can be bought in most food markets and gourmet food stores.

Dried fruit

This is a good source of protein, vitamins, and minerals in our diet. The best dried fruits are those dried in the traditional way in the warmth of the sun. You can now buy a wide range of dried fruit, including dried apples, apricots, bananas, dates, figs, grapes (currants, raisins, and golden raisins), mangoes, pears, nectarines, peaches, and plums (prunes). If the dried fruit is not guaranteed sun-dried, oil-free, and unsprayed, wash thoroughly in hot water before using.

Eggs

These are an important food for most vegetarians (with the exception of vegans). They are a good source of vitamins and minerals, and especially protein, as their balance of essential amino acids makes ninety-five percent of the protein available for the body to utilize. You may wish to avoid battery and factory farmed eggs if you have moral objections to battery farming of hens. When buying convenience foods and food products that contain eggs, check the labels to insure they are free-range.

Eggs are extremely versatile in vegetarian cookery. They can be eaten boiled, poached, scrambled,

fried, or as an essential ingredient in a whole range of savory and sweet dishes, from soufflés and quiches to omelets and cakes.

Fruit

Although we can now enjoy a wide range of fresh fruit year round, one of the delights of a healthy vegetarian diet is eating the new fruits as they come into season—the first strawberries of summer, apples and pears in the fall, tangerines at Christmas, and rosy pink rhubarb in the late spring. Fresh fruit is healthy, low in calories, a good source of vitamins, and a delicious way to end a meal. You will find some wonderful recipes in this book for fruit desserts. Choose firm, undamaged fruit with shining skin, and always wash it thoroughly before using as it may have been sprayed with insecticides. Better still, buy organically grown fruit if possible. These are now on sale in most food markets.

Gelatin

This gelling agent is made from animal ligaments, bones, skin, and tendons that have been boiled in water. Gelatin is present in many foods, including some margarines, ice creams, and low-fat yogurts, so you should always read labels carefully before buying these food products. You can use vegetarian alternatives, such as agar (which is derived from seaweed) instead.

Herbs

Fresh or dried, herbs can be used to flavor and enhance many vegetarian dishes. If you have a backyard, however small, it is a good idea to grow some herbs yourself. As well as the usual thyme, parsley, sage, rosemary, mint, and chives, you could experiment with dill weed, tarragon, cilantro, basil, fennel, marjoram, and savory. This will not only save you money buying small sachets of herbs in the food market but will also bring endless pleasure— a new dimension to your cooking and wonderful scents and aromas to your garden.

Honey

Honey is made by bees collecting the nectar from flowers, and the composition, flavor, and appearance of a particular type of honey will vary according to the flowers, the season, the weather, and the location. Honey contains vitamins B and C together with important minerals, and has long been used in medicine and healing. It can be used to replace sugar in many sweet dishes. However, it is avoided by most vegans.

Lentils

One of the oldest legumes, lentils are the small seeds of an Eastern Mediterranean plant. The most commonly used lentils are the orange-red Egyptian or Indian ones, but you can also buy the brownish-green lentils and little greenish-black Puy lentils, which are now becoming more fashionable. Unlike beans, lentils do not require soaking before cooking. For the vegetarian, they are a good source of protein (although they are not a complete protein). They can be used in soups, stews, curried Indian dishes, and salads.

Margarine

Vegetarians should note that many margarines contain animal fats, fish oils, E numbers, whey and gelatin (made from animal ligaments, tendons, and bones). Always look for pure vegetable oil margarines, which are now widely available in most food markets and stores.

Milk

Milk is full of goodness and an important natural ingredient in a well-balanced diet. Most vegetarians, with the exception of vegans, eat dairy foods (milk, cheese, and yogurt). Vegans can substitute soy milk. Cow's milk is a good source of protein, carbohydrates, calcium, other minerals, and vitamins. Although young children should have full-fat milk, many adults may prefer to use semi-skimmed or skimmed milk with their lower fat content. They can be substituted for full-fat milk in most recipes, but the results will not be so creamy.

Nuts

Nuts are exceptionally high in protein and form an important part of the vegetarian diet, although they do have a high fat content. Always try to buy organic nuts that have not been treated with preservatives. Almonds, Brazil nuts, cashews, coconut, hazelnuts, peanuts, pecans, pine nuts, pistachios, sweet chestnuts, and walnuts can all add interest and variety to our daily diet. The classic vegetarian dish utilizing nuts is nut roast, but you can also mix them into rice and pasta dishes, salads, and curries. They can be chopped or ground and mixed with flour and butter to make a "crumble" topping for savory dishes and desserts. When cooking with nuts, you should be aware that some people are allergic to them and you should check with your guests first.

Pasta

This is a marvelously versatile, healthy fast food that can be used in many vegetarian dishes—layered with vegetables and baked (as in lasagna and cannelloni), or tossed with fresh vegetable and cheese sauces. You can now buy a wide range of pasta, either fresh or dried, or you can make it yourself. Always cook pasta in plenty of lightly salted boiling water until it is just tender (*al dente*). It should never be soft or mushy, nor too firm and chewy.

Rice

Eaten throughout the world, rice contains starch, protein, B vitamins, and minerals. The best rice to eat is whole grain brown rice, which has a pleasantly nutty texture and flavor. However, white rice is the basis for most classic rice dishes, including risotto, paella, and pilafs. Use the plump Italian Arborio rice in risotto, and the fluffy Basmati rice for curries. Scented Thai jasmine rice is the perfect accompaniment to vegetable stir-fries. You can also

buy wild rice, which is not really a cereal at all but the green seeds of a wild grass. It is grown in the United States and harvested by the native Americans.

Seeds

Pumpkin, sesame, and sunflower seeds are all surprisingly rich in vitamins and minerals, and you should try to include them in your diet every day. You can eat them as a snack, scatter them over salads, or sprinkle them over bread loaves and rolls before baking. In the eastern Mediterranean, sesame seeds are ground into a paste and used in creamy tahini and hummus.

Spices

These add excitement and interest to many vegetarian dishes, both sweet and savory. If possible, use them freshly ground rather than buying them ready-ground. It really does make a difference to the flavor of a dish. You can grind them yourself in a pestle and mortar or an electric grinder. Many of the recipes in this book call for spices, especially allspice (berries), cinnamon (sticks), cloves, ground coriander, cumin, ginger (fresh root or dried), mace, nutmeg, pepper, and vanilla (extract or the bean).

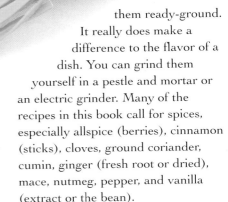

Vegetables

The most versatile and interesting of all foods, vegetables provide a rich source of nutrients in our diet— starch, protein, minerals, and vitamins. They come in such an enormous array of colors, textures, and flavors, from the more familiar root vegetables (potatoes, carrots, parsnips) and leafy green vegetables (cabbage, Brussels sprouts, spinach) to salad vegetables (lettuce, scallions,

tomatoes) and
the more exotic bell
peppers, eggplants, and
pumpkins. You can have fun
experimenting with so many
unusual vegetables, such as squash,
Swiss chard, exotic mushrooms,
sorrel, chayotes, and okra.

Always remember when buying
vegetables that they should look and
smell fresh, and have a bright,
wholesome appearance. They should
be firm and crisp, never dry or soft
with curling, wilted leaves. Many
stores now offer a good range of

organically grown vegetables, and
you should try to buy these, subject to
availability and budget. Always wash
vegetables thoroughly before using
to wash away dirt and traces
of sprays. The secret of
serving delicious
vegetables with
maximum nutritional
content is never to
overcook them.

Steaming above boiling
water is a good way of cooking
delicate vegetables, such as broccoli
and cauliflower florets, and also
insures minimal vitamin loss. If
boiling vegetables, cook them in the
minimum of water until they are just
tender but still retain some natural
crispness and bite. Keep the pan
uncovered to help retain their bright
green color. Stir-frying is another

excellent cooking method for bell
peppers, snow peas, scallions, and
green beans as the vegetables are
tossed and stirred quickly in a little oil
over high heat for only a few minutes.

Yogurt

Vegetarians should try to buy
organic yogurt, which is available in
most food markets and health stores.
Yogurt is an important healthy food
due to its ability to encourage
beneficial organisms to grow in the
intestine. The friendly lactobacillus
in the yogurt can help maintain the
balance of the intestinal microflora
and, indeed, manufactures many of
the B vitamins needed in the human
intestine to create a healthy
environment. You can buy yogurt or
make your own at home.

Cooking methods

Every vegetarian knows that the healthiest cooking methods, which retain maximum nutrients in our food, are steaming, grilling, broiling, and stir-frying. Vegetables respond well to these methods, and there are delicious recipes for broiled, barbecued, and stir-fried dishes in this book.

Grilling (or broiling)

Grilled food cooks rapidly when exposed to intense heat. The crisp, outer crust seals in moisture and helps retain nutrients, especially minerals and fat-soluble vitamins, which can be diminished by boiling, frying, or roasting. Grilling is a healthy, low-fat cooking method, as the food to be grilled is brushed only very lightly with the minimum of oil or marinade. Vegetables can be cooked under a conventional broiler, or, better still, over charcoal or wood. Grilling over hot coals imparts a delicious smoky flavor to the food.

Stir-frying

A quick and easy way of cooking vegetables in a minimum of oil in a wok or a large deep skillet. Stir-frying must always be performed over fierce heat to seal in the flavor of the vegetables as they come into contact with the hot wok. Foods to be stir-fried are always cut into thin strips or small pieces so that more of their surfaces are exposed to the oil and contact the wok, making them cook quickly. Timing is important as sometimes the food cooks in seconds rather than minutes, and although stir-fried vegetables should be just tender, they should retain their natural crispness and "bite." The best oils to use are sesame oil, peanut oil, or corn oil.

Steaming

This is a gentle, healthy way of cooking in which the food does not come into direct contact with the simmering water below but cooks in the steam. Many vegetables, especially the watery ones like zucchini, squash, and pumpkin, taste better steamed than boiled. Broccoli florets and snow peas are delicious steamed and retain their fresh green color. Timing is essential and it is important not to overcook steamed vegetables, so keep an eye on them and don't forget them. If you don't have a steamer, you can improvise with a large colander placed over a saucepan of simmering water and covered with a lid.

Roasting

Roasted seasonal vegetables are now extremely fashionable, but the tradition of roasting vegetables is very old. Root vegetables have long been cooked in Europe around the traditional roast, and the custom of roasting bell peppers, eggplants, onions, and tomatoes in olive oil has always been prevalent in the Spanish countryside. When roasting, always make sure that the oven is preheated to the correct temperature. Sprinkle the vegetables of your choice with good quality olive oil and scatter them with fresh herbs. If wished, you can tuck some garlic cloves down between the vegetables and then grind some sea salt and black pepper over the top. Delicious!

Frying

Although vegetable tempura, fritters, and croquettes taste wonderful, deep-frying in hot oil is not a very healthy way of cooking food that tends to absorb a lot of fat. Food to be deep-fried needs to be coated in flour, bread crumbs, or batter first to give it a protective covering. Always fry at 375°F, until crisp and golden, then remove with a slotted spoon and drain on absorbent paper towels to soak up excess oil before serving. Shallow frying uses less oil but, again, make sure that the oil is really hot before adding the food and drain it thoroughly on paper towels before serving.

Equipment

To be successful in vegetarian cookery, you need the right tools for the job. It is not necessary to invest in an expensive array of electronic gadgetry (juice extractors, ice-cream makers, pasta machines, etc.) but you should have the following:

- Sharp knives for cutting up vegetables, etc.
- Good quality heavy-based saucepans
- A wok for stir-frying
- A blender or food processor for puréeing soups, vegetables, etc.
- A steamer (optional) for steaming vegetables
- A cast-iron enameled casserole that can be used on top of the stove or in the oven
- Cookie sheets, quiche pans, and ovenproof dishes for baking and gratins
- A balloon whisk and electric hand whisk

Soups & Starters

Easy to make, filling and nutritious, many of these soups can be served with bread and cheese as a light meal. Alternatively, you can try one of the delicious vegetable first courses, including deep-fried snacks and fritters, stuffed vegetables, and blinis.

Cajun **Black Bean** Soup

The brilliant salsa garnish lifts this soup from the ordinary into the sublime. You can serve the salsa with Mexican or South-western food, or as a dip for tortilla chips and raw vegetables.

1 Soak the black beans in water overnight. Drain and rinse well under running cold water. Set aside.

2 Heat the olive oil in a large saucepan and fry the onion, carrot, leek, and garlic over gentle heat until softened. Add the chili.

3 Put the cumin and coriander seeds on a cookie sheet and roast in a preheated oven at 350°F for 5 minutes. Remove and grind to a powder in a pestle and mortar. Add to the vegetables in the pan.

4 Add the vegetable broth, the black beans, and tomato paste, stirring well. Bring to the boil, then reduce

1¹/₂ cups black beans
2 tablespoons olive oil
1 onion, chopped
1 carrot, diced
1 leek, trimmed and chopped
2 garlic cloves, minced
1 red chili, seeded and chopped
1 teaspoon cumin seeds
1 teaspoon coriander seeds
5 cups vegetable broth
3 tablespoons tomato paste
salt and freshly ground black pepper
sour cream, to garnish

FOR THE SALSA:
2 garlic cloves
3 tomatoes, skinned, seeded, and chopped
1 red onion, finely chopped
1 small red bell pepper, roasted, skinned, seeded, and chopped
1 red chili, seeded and finely chopped
2 tablespoons chopped fresh cilantro
juice of ¹/₂ lime
1 tablespoon olive oil
¹/₂ avocado, peeled and diced
freshly ground black pepper

the heat and simmer very gently for 2 hours. Take out some of the cooked black beans and set aside to use later in the salsa.

5 Purée the soup in a blender or food processor. Season to taste and reheat. Serve hot with the salsa and sour cream.

6 To make the salsa: roast the garlic cloves in their skins, then peel and

mash with a fork. Mix with the remaining ingredients.

Serves 6

Opposite: Cajun Black Bean Soup

Celery and Blue Cheese Soup

1¼ pounds celery, washed
and chopped
1 onion, finely chopped
2 tablespoons butter
4½ cups vegetable broth
few sprigs of thyme
4 ounces blue cheese
5/8 cup light cream
salt and freshly ground black pepper
herb croutons, to garnish
(see page 138)

Celery is one of the most subtly flavored vegetables and is ideally complimented by a creamy blue cheese. Together, they make a warming, delicious winter soup.

1 Fry the celery and onion in the butter over gentle heat, until they have softened. Make sure that the celery and onion do not color.

2 Add the vegetable broth and thyme, and bring to the boil.

Reduce the heat to a gentle simmer, cover the pan, and cook very gently for 20 minutes.

3 Purée the soup in a blender or food processor, then return to the pan. Crumble the blue cheese into the soup and heat very gently, stirring until the cheese melts into the soup. Stir in the cream and season to taste. Serve garnished with herb croutons.

Serves 4–6

Mushroom Soup

4 tablespoons butter
1 onion, chopped
2 garlic cloves, minced
½ pound white mushrooms,
thinly sliced
¼ pound exotic mushrooms
(chanterelles, morels, porcini),
thinly sliced
3¾ cups vegetable broth
pinch of nutmeg
5/8 cup milk
5 tablespoons Marsala
salt and freshly ground
black pepper
½ cup heavy cream or crème
fraîche

For this soup use oyster or shiitake mushrooms, or dried porcini that have been soaked in boiling water. Use the soaking liquid instead of broth.

1 Melt the butter in a large saucepan and fry the onion and garlic until translucent and soft. Stir in the mushrooms and then cook gently for about 5 minutes.

2 Add the hot vegetable broth and a pinch of nutmeg. Bring to a simmer, stir in the milk and Marsala, and then simmer gently for 45 minutes, stirring occasionally.

3 Remove a few of the mushrooms with a slotted spoon and set aside for the garnish. Purée the soup in a blender or food processor and return to the pan. Season to taste, stir in the cream or crème fraîche and reheat gently. Serve in soup bowls, garnished with the reserved mushrooms.

Serves 6

Tuscan **Bean** Soup

1½ cups dried cannellini or white
beans
5 tablespoons olive oil
1 onion, chopped
1 leek, washed, trimmed,
and chopped
2 carrots, chopped
2 stalks celery, chopped
2 potatoes, cubed
1 bulb fennel, chopped (optional)
1 cup skinned and chopped
tomatoes
2 garlic cloves, minced
5 cups vegetable broth
1 pound dark green cabbage,
shredded
salt and freshly ground
black pepper

TO GARNISH:
6 slices crusty white bread
1–2 garlic cloves, peeled
olive oil

A thick, robust peasant soup, in Tuscany this is known as *la Ribollita*, and it is made overnight. To be authentic, it must be made with white cannellini beans and cabbage. In Italy, they use *cavolo nero*, but you can cheat with a dark green cabbage, some greens, or even Swiss chard.

1 Soak the beans in cold water overnight, or for at least 5 hours. Drain and rinse the beans under running cold water.

2 Heat the olive oil in a large saucepan and add the onion, leek, carrots, celery, potatoes, fennel, and tomatoes. Stew the vegetables gently in the olive oil for 8–10 minutes. Stir in the garlic and cook for 2 minutes.

3 Add the vegetable broth and the drained beans, bring to the boil, then reduce the heat to a simmer. Cook very gently for 1 hour and then stir in the cabbage. Continue cooking for 15–20 minutes, until the beans are cooked and tender.

4 Season the soup to taste with salt and pepper, remove from the heat, and cover the pan with a lid. Let stand in a cool place until the next day.

5 The following day, reheat the soup, and meanwhile prepare the garnish. Rub the slices of bread with the garlic cloves and brush lightly with a little olive oil. Place under a hot broiler to toast them.

6 Ladle the soup into bowls and top each one with a slice of toasted garlic bread. Serve with a small jug of olive oil for people to trickle over the top of their soup, if wished.

Serves 4

Pumpkin Soup

2 onions, finely chopped
2 garlic cloves, minced
3 tablespoons olive oil
3 pound wedge of pumpkin
3¾ cups vegetable broth
1 teaspoon chopped fresh sage
pinch of sugar
salt and freshly ground
black pepper
½ cup grated Cheddar or
Monterey Jack cheese
garlic croutons, to garnish
(see page 138)

This is a traditional French country soup, but you can easily transform it into a West Indian favorite by leaving out the cheese and stirring in a dash of hot pepper sauce just before serving.

1 Fry the onions and garlic in the olive oil in a large saucepan over low heat until soft and translucent.

2 Remove the seeds from the pumpkin and cut off the rind. Cut the flesh of the pumpkin into small cubes and add to the onions in the pan. Cook gently for 5 minutes.

3 Add the vegetable broth, sage, and sugar, and simmer over low heat for 30–40 minutes, until the pumpkin is tender and starts to break up.

4 Purée the soup in a blender or food processor until smooth. Return to the pan and reheat. Season to taste with salt and pepper, and serve the soup sprinkled with grated cheese and garlic croutons.

Serves 6

Spicy Carrot and Cumin Soup

A great soup for warming you up on a cold winter's evening. You can vary the flavor by substituting parsnip for some of the carrot.

2 tablespoons butter
1¼ pounds carrots, diced
1 onion, finely chopped
2 garlic cloves, minced
1 potato, diced
½ teaspoon ground cumin
½ teaspoon ground nutmeg
pinch each of ground ginger, turmeric, and paprika
¼ teaspoon ground coriander
1 teaspoon soft brown sugar
3¾ cups vegetable broth
salt and pepper
⅝ cup milk
plain yogurt and chopped parsley or cilantro, to garnish

1 Melt the butter in a large saucepan and stir in the carrots, onion, garlic, and potato. Cook gently over low heat until softened.

2 Stir in all the spices and cook over low heat for 2–3 minutes. Add the brown sugar and vegetable broth and bring to the boil. Reduce the heat immediately and simmer for 15–20 minutes, until tender.

3 Purée the soup in a blender or food processor until it has a smooth texture. Return to the pan, season to taste and stir in the milk. Reheat the soup over low heat.

4 Serve the soup topped with a swirl of yogurt and garnish with a sprinkling of parsley or cilantro.

Serves 6

Soupe au Pistou

This is the ultimate in bean and vegetable soups—a simple Provençal clear soup made special by the addition of garlicky pistou sauce stirred in at the table. For the best results, make the pistou yourself and don't be tempted to buy a ready made pesto from the food market.

1½ cups dried white beans
2 tablespoons olive oil
2 carrots, diced
2 leeks, trimmed and diced
2 stalks celery, diced
¾ pound tomatoes, skinned and chopped
5 cups water
2 large potatoes, peeled and diced
½ pound thin green beans, trimmed and cut into ½-inch lengths
½ pound zucchini, diced
½ cup vermicelli or tiny soup pasta
salt and freshly ground black pepper

FOR THE PISTOU:
4 garlic cloves, peeled
pinch of salt
20–25 basil leaves
1 cup grated vegetarian Parmesan cheese
½ cup olive oil

1 Put the beans in a bowl, cover with cold water and soak overnight. Drain the beans and put them in a large saucepan. Cover with plenty of fresh water and bring to a boil. Boil for 10 minutes, skimming off any scum that rises to the surface. Simmer for 1 hour until the beans are tender, then drain.

2 Heat the olive oil in a large saucepan and stir in the carrots, leeks, celery, and tomatoes. Cook gently for 2–3 minutes. Add the water and bring to the boil. Reduce the heat and simmer for 15 minutes.

3 Add the potatoes, green beans, zucchini, and vermicelli, and simmer gently for about 15 minutes. The vegetables should be tender but still retain their shape. Season to taste with salt and pepper.

4 While the soup is cooking, make the pistou. Put the garlic, salt, and basil in a blender or food processor and process to a purée. Add the Parmesan cheese, process again, and then add the olive oil through the feed tube in a thin steady trickle until the mixture is well blended. You should end up with a thick bright green paste. Transfer to a bowl.

5 Stir the pistou into the soup just before serving, or serve it separately and let your guests help themselves. Serve with crusty bread.

Serves 6

Spicy **Callaloo**

In the West Indies, this soup is made with fresh callaloo leaves, which are sometimes available in specialist Caribbean stores. Spinach makes a good substitute.

1 pound fresh callaloo or
spinach leaves
1 large onion, finely chopped
2 garlic cloves, minced
3 tablespoons peanut or olive oil
1 red chili, seeded and
finely chopped
1 teaspoon turmeric

1/2 pound fresh okra, trimmed
and thinly sliced
3 3/4 cups vegetable broth
few strands of saffron
2 cups coconut milk
salt and freshly ground black pepper
juice of 1/2 lime
dash of hot pepper sauce

1 Wash the callaloo or spinach leaves thoroughly to remove any dirt. Drain well, shake dry, and discard any tough stems. Chop the leaves and set aside.

2 Fry the onion and garlic in the peanut or olive oil in a large saucepan. Cook for 5 minutes until soft and translucent. Stir in the chili and turmeric and cook for 1–2 minutes.

3 Add the okra and the callaloo or spinach leaves and stir over medium heat until the leaves start to wilt and turn bright green. Add the vegetable broth and saffron and bring to a simmer. Cover the pan and simmer for 20 minutes.

4 Stir in the coconut milk and continue cooking for 5–10 minutes. Season to taste and, just before serving, stir in the lime juice and a dash of hot pepper sauce.

Serves 6

Moroccan **Harira**

This colorful soup is traditionally made during Ramadan and is always consumed at sunset when the daily fast comes to an end. It is both refreshing and comforting. Harissa is a hot spice mixture.

1 cup dried garbanzo peas
3 tablespoons olive oil
1 onion, chopped
1 stalk celery, chopped
1 teaspoon ground
cinnamon
1 teaspoon turmeric
1 teaspoon paprika
1 pound tomatoes, skinned
and chopped
2/3 cup red lentils
5 cups vegetable broth
1/2 cup vermicelli
salt and freshly ground
black pepper
few sprigs of fresh
cilantro, chopped
few sprigs of flat-leaf
parsley, chopped
lemon wedges and harissa
(optional), to serve

1 Put the garbanzo peas in a bowl, cover with cold water, and soak overnight. The following day, drain them and rinse under running cold water. Set aside.

2 Heat the oil in a large saucepan and cook the onion and celery over low heat until softened. Stir in the spices and cook for 2–3 minutes. Add the tomatoes and lentils and stir well.

3 Add the garbanzo peas and cook gently for about 5 minutes. Add the vegetable broth and then simmer gently for 1 1/2–2 hours, until the garbanzo peas are tender.

4 Add the vermicelli and simmer for a further 15 minutes. Season to taste with salt and pepper, and stir in the chopped cilantro and parsley. Serve hot with lemon wedges and a little bowl of harissa (optional).

Serves 6

Dolmades

Serves 6

Lemon-scented vine leaves rolled around a spicy rice stuffing are a traditional Middle Eastern *meze*. If you have a vine in your backyard, you can enjoy the luxury of using fresh leaves. However, most of us will have to fall back on pickled or canned ones, which are now widely available from most food markets and or gourmet food stores.

6 ounces fresh or pickled vine leaves
1/2 cup long-grain rice
1 small onion, finely chopped
1 tomato, skinned, seeded, and chopped
few sprigs of parsley, finely chopped
1 tablespoon chopped mint
1 tablespoon chopped chives
1/4 teaspoon each of ground cinnamon, allspice, and cumin
2 tablespoons pine nuts
1/2 cup currants
salt and freshly ground black pepper
2 garlic cloves, sliced
4 tablespoons olive oil
5/8 cup water
1 teaspoon sugar
juice of 1 lemon
olive oil and lemon juice, to serve

Line the base of a heavy saucepan with any broken or leftover leaves and pack in the dolmades tightly in layers. Tuck the sliced garlic in between the dolmades.

4 Pour in the olive oil, water, sugar, and lemon juice, press a plate down over the top and cover the pan with a lid. Simmer gently for 1¹/₂ hours, checking from time to time and adding more boiling water if necessary, as it is absorbed by the filling. Leave in the pan to cool before removing the dolmades. Serve cold, dressed with a little olive oil and lemon juice.

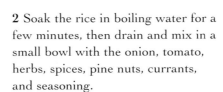

1 If you are using fresh vine leaves, boil them for 3–4 minutes in water and then drain. Pickled vine leaves should be soaked in hot water for 20–30 minutes, then removed and patted dry with paper towels. Remove the stalks from the leaves and spread them out with the veined underside facing upward.

2 Soak the rice in boiling water for a few minutes, then drain and mix in a small bowl with the onion, tomato, herbs, spices, pine nuts, currants, and seasoning.

3 Place a little of the filling in the center of each leaf, fold the sides over into the middle, and roll up.

Mushrooms on Polenta Croutes

This is a spectacular way to serve creamed mushrooms—on crisp golden polenta rectangles. You can serve the croutes as a first course, or as a light meal with a crisp green salad.

2 tablespoons butter
1 small onion, finely chopped
1 pound button mushrooms, quartered
$^{1}/_{2}$ cup Madeira or Marsala
1 cup heavy cream
squeeze of lemon juice
salt and freshly ground black pepper
1 tablespoon chopped parsley

FOR THE CROUTES:
$3^{3}/_{4}$ cups water
salt
1 cup polenta
2 tablespoons sweet butter
olive oil for frying

1 Make the polenta croutes: bring the water and salt to the boil in a large saucepan. Gradually add the polenta in a steady, thin stream, beating all the time. Reduce the heat to a bare simmer—as low as it will go—and continue stirring and beating the polenta with a wooden spoon for about 15 minutes, until the polenta is thick and smooth and has absorbed all the liquid. It should leave the sides of the pan clean.

2 Stir in the butter thoroughly and pour the polenta into an oiled rectangular pan. Smooth the surface and set aside to cool.

3 When cold, cut the polenta into 12 rectangles. Heat the olive oil and fry the polenta croûtes on both sides until crisp and golden. Drain on paper towels and keep warm while you prepare the mushroom topping.

4 Melt the butter and gently cook the onion until soft and golden. Add the mushrooms and cook until lightly golden. Add the Madeira or Marsala and cook rapidly until the liquid evaporates and turns syrupy. Stir in the cream and simmer until the sauce thickens. Season with lemon juice and salt and pepper.

5 Top the polenta croutes with the creamed mushrooms and serve sprinkled with chopped parsley.

Serves 4

Sicilian Caponata

3 eggplants, cut into $^{1}/_{2}$-inch dice
1 onion, thinly sliced
4 tablespoons olive oil
2 stalks celery, diced
$^{5}/_{8}$ cup passata (sieved tomatoes)
3 tablespoons wine vinegar
1 tablespoon sugar
1 red bell pepper, seeded and thinly sliced

1 yellow bell pepper, seeded and thinly sliced
$^{1}/_{4}$ cup capers, coarsely chopped
$^{1}/_{2}$ cup black olives, pitted
$^{1}/_{2}$ cup green olives, pitted
2 tablespoons pine nuts
salt and freshly ground black pepper
2 tablespoons chopped parsley

This is the Sicilian "sweet and sour" way of cooking eggplants with bell peppers, capers, and olives. It makes a wonderful first course for summer entertaining. The flavors improve if it is made the day before it is eaten.

1 Put the eggplants in a colander, sprinkle with salt, and set aside for 20 minutes to drain and exude their bitter juices. Rinse well under running cold water and pat dry with paper towels.

2 Fry the onion in the olive oil until soft and translucent. Add the celery and cook for 3 minutes to soften. Stir in the eggplant and cook, stirring occasionally, for a few more minutes.

3 Add the passata, wine vinegar, sugar, red and yellow bell peppers,

capers, olives, and pine nuts, and cook gently over low heat until the vegetables are tender. Season to taste with salt and pepper.

4 Transfer the mixture to a serving dish and set aside to cool. The caponata is best when eaten at room

Mushrooms on Polenta Croutes

temperature rather than being served cold straight from the refrigerator. Serve it sprinkled with some chopped parsley.

Serves 4

Blinis with Sun-dried Tomatoes

1 cup buckwheat flour
1 cup white flour
1 teaspoon salt
1$^{1}/_{2}$ cups warm milk
$^{1}/_{2}$ ounce fresh yeast
1 teaspoon sugar
2 eggs, separated
2 tablespoons sour cream
sweet butter for frying

FOR THE TOPPING:
$^{1}/_{4}$ stick butter, melted
$^{1}/_{2}$ red onion, finely chopped
1 ounce sun-dried tomatoes,
cut into slivers
freshly ground black pepper
sour cream and chopped
chives, to garnish

What could be more opulent than traditional Russian blinis topped with melted butter, diced onion, sun-dried tomatoes, and a generous spoonful of sour cream? For an alternative, try thinly sliced avocado and creamy goat's cheese.

1 Sift the flours and salt into a mixing bowl. Heat the milk to lukewarm, and crumble in the yeast. Add the sugar and egg yolks and stir well. Make a hollow in the center of the flours and pour in the yeast mixture and sour cream. Mix well.

2 Cover the bowl and leave in a warm place for about 1 hour, until the batter gets thicker and some bubbles appear on the surface.

3 Beat the egg whites until stiff and gently fold into the batter.

4 Heat a small amount of butter in a non-stick skillet and pour in 2 tablespoons of the batter. Fry until the underside is set and golden. Flip over and cook the other side. Cook the remaining blinis in the same way and keep warm until required.

5 Serve the blinis warm with melted butter, red onion, sun-dried tomatoes, and a good grinding of black pepper. Top with a spoonful of sour cream and some chopped chives.

Serves 6

Trio of Stuffed Vegetables

Stuffed colorful vegetables are a feature of Mediterranean cooking and make a delicious first course. Serve them hot or cold with a garnish of crisp bitter salad leaves.

1 Cut the eggplants, bell peppers, and zucchini in half lengthwise. Scoop out the flesh from the eggplants and zucchini and chop roughly. Remove the seeds from the bell peppers.

2 Heat 3 tablespoons of the olive oil and sauté the onion and garlic until soft and translucent. Add the eggplant and zucchini flesh, and cook gently until soft and golden.

3 Remove from the heat and stir in the tomatoes, bread crumbs, pine

2 eggplants
1 large yellow bell pepper
1 large red bell pepper
2 zucchini
7 tablespoons extra-virgin olive oil
1 onion, finely chopped
2 garlic cloves, minced
$^{3}/_{4}$ pound tomatoes, skinned
and chopped

1 cup fresh white bread crumbs
2 tablespoons pine nuts
2 tablespoons chopped capers
$^{1}/_{3}$ cup grated Parmesan cheese
2 tablespoons chopped parsley
or marjoram
salt and freshly ground black pepper
arugula, watercress, and radicchio,
to garnish

nuts, capers, Parmesan cheese, herbs and seasoning to taste.

4 Fill the eggplant, bell pepper, and zucchini shells with the stuffing mixture, smoothing the tops. Arrange in a well-oiled baking pan and then sprinkle the remaining olive oil over the top.

5 Bake the stuffed vegetables in a preheated oven at 400°F for about 45 minutes, until golden brown. Take care that they do not burn. Serve warm or cold with a garnish of salad leaves, such as arugula, watercress, and radicchio.

Serves 6

Char-grilled **Bell Pepper** Salad

4 red, green, and yellow bell
peppers

FOR THE OLIVE OIL
DRESSING:
4 tablespoons olive oil
2 garlic cloves, minced
freshly ground sea salt and
black pepper
2 tablespoons chopped parsley

FOR THE SALSA VERDE:
^{2}/$_3$ cup capers, chopped
2 garlic cloves, minced
2 teaspoons whole grain
Dijon mustard
6 tablespoons olive oil
2 tablespoons white wine vinegar
2 tablespoons chopped marjoram
3 tablespoons chopped parsley
salt and freshly ground
black pepper

Grilling brings out the natural sweetness and juiciness of bell peppers.
You can cook the bell peppers under a broiler or, better still, grill them
over hot coals until the skin is charred. Serve with a simple dressing of
olive oil and garlic or a piquant salsa verde.

1 Place the bell peppers under a hot
broiler and cook them, turning
occasionally, until they are charred
and blistered. Remove and place in a
plastic bag. Leave to cool, then peel
away the skins.

2 Cut the bell peppers open and
remove the seeds. Cut the flesh into
strips and arrange in a serving dish.
Sprinkle with olive oil and garlic.
Season with salt and pepper and
scatter the parsley over the top.

3 Alternatively, serve the bell
peppers warm with the salsa verde.
To make the salsa verde, mix all the
ingredients together until well

blended. Spoon a little over the bell
peppers and serve the rest separately.
Eat with crusty bread.

Serves 4–6

Deep-fried **Camembert**

These little golden fritters, oozing with melted cheese, can be served in the French style with a salad of
dressed bitter leaves, some olives and baby gherkins, or with a fresh, tart cranberry sauce.

2 boxes just ripe Camembert
cheese
1 large egg, beaten
1 tablespoon flour
2 cups fresh bread crumbs
vegetable oil, for deep-frying

FOR THE CRANBERRY SAUCE:
1 cup water
^{1}/$_3$ cup sugar
2 cups fresh cranberries
juice of 1 orange

1 Make the cranberry sauce. Put the
water and sugar in a saucepan and
stir over low heat until the sugar
dissolves. Bring to a boil and add the
cranberries. Bring back to a boil,
then simmer for 5 minutes, until the
berries start popping. Cover the pan
and set aside to cool. When cold and
thick, stir the orange juice into the
sauce. Refrigerate until required.

2 Cut each Camembert cheese into 6
triangles. Dip them in the beaten
egg, shaking off any excess, and then
into the flour and bread crumbs.

3 Heat the vegetable oil in a large,
heavy saucepan or deep-fat fryer to
375°F, and quickly fry the bread-
crumbed Camembert triangles, a few
at a time, until crisp and golden
brown. Remove with a slotted spoon,
drain on paper towels, and keep
warm while you fry the remaining
triangles in the same way.

4 Serve the Camembert immediately
with the cranberry sauce and a
garnish of bitter salad leaves.

Serves 4

Falafel Snacks

3 cups canned garbanzos
1 onion, finely chopped
4 garlic cloves, minced
1 teaspoon ground cumin
1 teaspoon ground coriander
1 small red chili, seeded and finely chopped (optional)
2 tablespoons all-purpose flour
1/4 teaspoon baking powder
1 tablespoon chopped fresh cilantro

2 tablespoons chopped parsley
salt and freshly ground black pepper
oil for deep-frying

TO SERVE:
2/3 cup plain yogurt
3 tablespoons chopped mint
tahini
lemon wedges

These crisp, spicy snacks are popular street food in Israel and throughout the Middle East. To be authentic, you should use dried garbanzos and soak them overnight, but this is both tedious and time-consuming for busy cooks. This quick and simple recipe uses canned garbanzo peas to make your life easier.

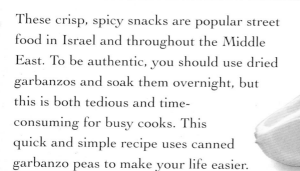

1 Drain the garbanzos and rinse in a colander under running cold water. Dry on paper towels and put into a food processor with the onion, garlic, cumin, ground coriander, and chili, if using. Process until thick and smooth. Add the flour, baking powder, herbs, and seasoning, and process quickly until well blended.

2 Transfer the mixture to a bowl, and then roll between your floured hands into little balls. Deep-fry the falafel in hot oil until golden brown and crisp. Remove with a slotted spoon and drain on paper towels.

3 Serve hot with a bowl of yogurt blended with chopped mint, or some tahini and lemon wedges.

Serves 4

Feta Cheese Pastries

14 ounce packet of filo pastry
6 tablespoons butter, melted

FOR THE FILLING:
2 eggs, lightly beaten
6 ounces feta cheese, crumbled
1 cup grated Swiss or vegetarian Parmesan cheese
2 tablespoons chopped flat-leaf parsley
freshly ground black pepper
freshly grated nutmeg

These little Greek pastries oozing with feta cheese melt in the mouth and can be served as a first course or as canapés with drinks. They can be made in advance and then reheated in a low oven.

1 Make the feta cheese filling. Mix the beaten eggs with the cheeses, parsley, black pepper, and nutmeg. Do not add any salt as the feta is salty enough.

2 Take one of the filo pastry sheets and brush lightly with melted butter. Cut the sheet into 3 long strips. Fold each strip over lengthwise and brush with more butter. Place a small spoonful of the filling at one end of the strip and fold the pastry over to make a triangle. Fold over again in this way, and continue folding until

the strip is used up and you have a thick triangle. Brush with more melted butter and place on a greased cookie sheet. Make the remaining pastries in the same way.

3 Cook in a preheated oven at 375°F for 15–20 minutes, until the pastries are crisp and golden. Serve them immediately.

Serves 8-12

Opposite: Feta Cheese Pastries and Falafel Snacks

Pasta

Pasta is the perfect vegetarian food—healthy, filling and infinitely versatile. Not only are there many different types and shapes of pasta, but there are also endless flavorings and delicious sauces that you can serve with them. In this chapter, you will find recipes for classic filled and baked pasta dishes, quick pasta suppers, gnocchi, and polenta.

Ravioli with Sage

The best ravioli is made with homemade pasta, but if you haven't got the time or the inclination to make it yourself, you can buy some sheets of fresh readymade lasagna from a food market or gourmet food store and use them instead. You can use this basic recipe for pasta to make tagliatelle, lasagna, cannelloni, and other types of pasta. To vary the flavor and color of the pasta, try adding one of the following when making the dough: some finely chopped herbs, some cooked chopped spinach, or a tablespoon of tomato paste.

FOR THE HOMEMADE PASTA:
2³/₄ cups white flour
pinch of salt
3 eggs
1 tablespoon olive oil
flour for dusting
4 tablespoons butter, melted
few fresh sage leaves, torn
grated vegetarian Parmesan cheese

FOR THE FILLING:
1¹/₃ cups ricotta cheese
2 tablespoons pesto sauce
1 egg yolk
salt and freshly ground
black pepper

1 Make the pasta: sift the flour and salt into a mixing bowl. Make a hollow in the center and add the eggs. Draw the flour in from the sides and mix well. Add the olive oil and continue mixing with your hands until you have a soft, pliable dough.

2 Knead the dough on a lightly floured surface for 5–10 minutes, until silky and elastic. Leave to rest in a cool place for 15 minutes.

3 Roll out the dough on a lightly floured surface, rolling and stretching it until it is really thin. Leave it for about 10 minutes to rest and dry out before using.

4 Mix all the filling ingredients together in a bowl. Cut the dough in half and trim the edges, so that you have 2 large squares. Mark one half into smaller squares and then drop teaspoonfuls of the filling into the marked squares.

5 Cover with the other sheet of pasta, and press gently around each little mound of filling with your fingertips. Cut the pasta into squares with a pastry cutter wheel.

6 Bring a large pan of lightly salted water to the boil and drop in the ravioli squares. Cook for about 5 minutes, until the ravioli rise to the surface and are tender (*al dente*). Remove with a slotted spoon and drain well.

7 Serve the ravioli with melted butter, sprinkled with sage, black pepper, and Parmesan cheese.

Serves 4

Opposite: Ravioli with Sage

Cannelloni with Tomato Sauce

1 quantity fresh pasta (see page 30)
or 16 cannelloni tubes
5 tablespoons light cream
2 tablespoons grated vegetarian
Parmesan cheese

FOR THE FILLING:
10 ounces fresh spinach, washed and
tough stalks removed
1 1/2 cups ricotta cheese
1 teaspoon freshly grated nutmeg
salt and freshly ground black pepper
2 egg yolks

2 tablespoons grated vegetarian
Parmesan cheese

FOR THE TOMATO SAUCE:
2 tablespoons olive oil
1 onion, finely chopped
2 garlic cloves, minced
1 1/2 cups canned chopped tomatoes
1 teaspoon tomato paste
few basil leaves, chopped
1 teaspoon sugar
salt and freshly ground
black pepper

Pasta tubes filled with spinach and ricotta make a substantial supper dish. You can use either fresh pasta or the readymade tubes.

1 Make the tomato sauce: heat the oil and fry the onion and garlic until soft and translucent. Add the tomatoes and tomato paste and simmer gently for 10–15 minutes, until thickened. Add the basil, sugar, and salt and pepper to taste.

2 Make the filling: put the spinach leaves in a large saucepan with 1–2 tablespoons of water. Cover with a lid and cook gently over very low heat for about 5 minutes, until the leaves go limp and give out their juice. Drain the spinach in a colander, pressing down well with a small plate or saucer to squeeze out any excess moisture.

3 Chop the spinach roughly and mix in a bowl with the ricotta cheese, nutmeg, seasoning, egg yolks, and Parmesan cheese.

4 Cut the fresh pasta (if using) into large squares, and divide the filling between them. Roll up into cylinder shapes. Alternatively, if you are using readymade cannelloni tubes, spoon the filling into the tubes.

5 Arrange the cannelloni in an oiled ovenproof dish and pour the tomato sauce over them. Spoon the cream over the top and then sprinkle with Parmesan cheese. Bake in a preheated oven at 400°F for about 20 minutes, until golden brown.

Serves 4

Deluxe Macaroni and Cheese

4 tablespoons butter
2 leeks, washed, trimmed, and
sliced diagonally
2 zucchini, sliced
1/4 cup sun-dried tomatoes
in oil, thinly sliced
1/2 pound macaroni
2 tablespoons grated Cheddar or
Monterey Jack cheese
1 tablespoon fresh white bread
crumbs
1 tablespoon butter
1 tablespoon chopped parsley

FOR THE SAUCE:
2 tablespoons butter
2–3 tablespoons flour
2 1/2 cups milk
1 teaspoon Dijon mustard
good pinch of paprika
1 cup grated Monterey Jack or
Cheddar cheese
1/2 cup crumbled blue cheese,
salt and freshly ground
black pepper

Here's a luxurious version of the traditional macaroni in plain cheese sauce. This Macaroni and Cheese has been made special by the addition of sun-dried tomatoes, leeks, zucchini, and blue cheese. You could try some other variations by adding some sautéed sliced mushrooms or onions, chopped tomatoes, or scallions.

1 Melt the butter and gently fry the leeks and zucchini until softened and slightly colored. Stir in the sun-dried

tomatoes and then remove the pan from the heat.

2 Meanwhile, cook the macaroni in a large pan of lightly salted boiling water for about 10 minutes, until tender. Drain well.

3 Make the sauce: melt the butter and stir in the flour. Cook gently for 1 minute, then gradually add the milk, stirring all the time, until the sauce is thick and smooth. Stir in the mustard, paprika, and cheeses, and simmer gently for 2–3 minutes. Season to taste.

4 Mix together the cooked macaroni and vegetables and put into a buttered one-quart ovenproof dish. Pour the cheese sauce over the top. Sprinkle with the grated Monterey Jack or Cheddar cheese and bread crumbs, and then dot the top with butter.

5 Bake the Macaroni and Cheese in a preheated oven at 350°F for 20–30 minutes, until the top is crisp and golden brown. Sprinkle with parsley and serve immediately.

Serves 4

Spaghetti Napoletana

This is one of the simplest pasta dishes you can make—just spaghetti tossed in a fresh tomato sauce. For a stronger, more fiery flavor, add a couple of finely chopped fresh red chilies and you will have a classic arrabbiata sauce.

3/4 **pound spaghetti**
1/3 **cup grated vegetarian Parmesan or Pecorino cheese**

FOR THE SAUCE:
5 **tablespoons olive oil**
1 **large onion, finely chopped**
2 **garlic cloves, minced**
1 **pound plum tomatoes, skinned and chopped**

(or 1 1/2 **cups passata**)
2 **tablespoons tomato paste**
1 **teaspoon sugar**
1/2 **cup dry white wine**
1 **tablespoon finely chopped parsley**
few basil leaves, torn
salt and freshly ground black pepper
a few ripe black olives, pitted (optional)

---

1 To make the sauce, heat the olive oil and gently fry the onion and garlic until soft and lightly colored. Add the tomatoes, tomato paste, sugar, and white wine. Simmer gently for about 15 minutes, until the tomato sauce has thickened and reduced a little. Stir in the chopped parsley and basil and then season to taste with salt and pepper. Add the olives, if using.

2 While the sauce is cooking, bring a large saucepan of salted water to the boil and add the spaghetti. Boil rapidly for 8–10 minutes, until the pasta is cooked and *al dente* (tender to the bite). Drain well.

3 Toss the pasta in the tomato sauce and serve immediately, sprinkled with Parmesan or Pecorino cheese. A crisp salad of bitter leaves in a mustardy vinaigrette dressing makes a good accompaniment.

Serves 4

Roasted Vegetable Lasagna

Serves 6

Use the dried lasagna sheets that do not require precooking. Roasting the vegetables adds sweetness and a new dimension to this dish. If it's more convenient, you can prepare the lasagna a few hours ahead or even the previous day, and refrigerate it until you are ready to cook the meal.

10–12 sheets lasagna
1 quantity tomato sauce (see page 32)
2 tablespoons grated vegetarian Parmesan cheese

FOR THE ROASTED VEGETABLES:
1 red bell pepper, seeded and cubed
1 green bell pepper, seeded and cubed
1 small eggplant, cubed
1 onion, thickly sliced and cubed
1 red onion, thickly sliced and cubed
2 zucchini, sliced

1 garlic clove, minced
1 tablespoon chopped mixed herbs
3 tablespoons olive oil
salt and freshly ground black pepper

FOR THE WHITE SAUCE:
2 tablespoons butter
2 tablespoons flour
2 1/2 cups milk
pinch of grated nutmeg
salt and freshly ground black pepper

1 Prepare the vegetables and arrange them in a baking pan. Sprinkle with the minced garlic and herbs and toss lightly in the olive oil. Season with salt and pepper. Cook in a preheated oven at 400°F for about 30 minutes, until the vegetables are tender and just beginning to char.

2 Meanwhile, make the white sauce. Melt the butter and stir in the flour. Cook over low heat for 2–3 minutes, then gradually add the milk, beating well after each addition, until the sauce is thick and smooth. Season with nutmeg and salt and pepper, reduce the heat and cook gently for 2 minutes.

3 Assemble the lasagna in a large buttered ovenproof dish. Cover the base with a layer of tomato sauce and then a layer of the roasted vegetables. Cover with sheets of lasagna, and spread some white sauce over the top. Continue layering up in this way, finishing with a layer of lasagna topped with white sauce.

4 Sprinkle with Parmesan cheese and bake in a preheated oven at 375°F for 20–25 minutes, until the top is crisp and golden. Cut the lasagna into portions and serve hot with a crisp salad.

Pasta Primavera

This is a great "green" dish to serve in early summer when there are so many fresh seasonal vegetables to choose from. You need not slavishly follow the recipe given here—experiment with whatever vegetables are available. Thin green beans, snow peas, Swiss chard and shredded cabbage can all be added to the pasta.

1 Make the herb butter: beat the softened butter with the herbs and set aside.

³/4 pound fine asparagus, trimmed and sliced diagonally
2 cups fresh peas, shelled
³/4 pound fava beans, shelled
4 baby zucchini, sliced diagonally
3 tablespoons fruity green olive oil
1 garlic clove, minced
4 scallions, coarsely chopped
salt and freshly ground black pepper

1 pound angel hair pasta
grated vegetarian Parmesan cheese, to serve

FOR THE HERB BUTTER:
2 tablespoons sweet butter, softened
1 tablespoon finely chopped parsley
1 tablespoon chopped chives

2 Cook the asparagus, peas, fava beans, and zucchini in lightly salted boiling water for 1 minute. Drain well in a colander.

3 Heat the olive oil in a large skillet, add the garlic, and cook gently for 1–2 minutes. Add all the drained cooked vegetables and the scallions, and then gently toss in the olive oil over low heat for a few minutes, until they are just tender. Season to taste with salt and pepper.

4 Meanwhile, cook the pasta in lightly salted boiling water until just tender (al dente). Drain and toss with the vegetables and herb butter. Serve the pasta immediately, sprinkled with a little Parmesan cheese.

Serves 4

Pasta with Mushrooms

This is an easy dish that you can create in less than half an hour when you rush in from work at the end of a busy day. You can use literally any dried pasta that you can find in the cupboard, but the broad noodles called pappardelle are particularly good. If you don't have many fresh mushrooms, use some dried porcini instead.

1 Heat the olive oil and butter in a large skillet, and stir in the mushrooms. Cook gently over low heat until the mushrooms soften and start to turn golden.

1 tablespoon olive oil
4 tablespoons butter
1 pound mixed fresh mushrooms, sliced (e.g., open cap, morels, chanterelles, porcini, cèpes, or even button)
⁵/8 cup dry white wine

¹/2 cup heavy cream
salt and freshly ground black pepper
³/4 pound dried pappardelle or fettuccine
2 tablespoons vegetarian Parmesan cheese
2 tablespoons chopped parsley

2 Pour in the white wine and turn up the heat. Let the wine bubble and reduce down until it is almost syrupy. Stir in the cream and heat through gently. Season with salt and pepper.

3 Meanwhile, cook the pasta in lightly salted boiling water until it is tender (al dente). Drain well and add to the skillet of mushroom sauce.

4 Toss lightly together and serve immediately, sprinkled with shavings of fresh Parmesan cheese and chopped parsley.

Serves 4

Florentine Pasta

This is the ultimate in healthy fast food—a vibrant dish that can be cooked in minutes. The arugula adds a slightly bitter taste to the creamy blue cheese and spinach sauce. If possible, use Gorgonzola cheese.

1 pound fresh spinach
2 ounces arugula
4 tablespoons milk
1 tablespoon butter
8 ounces blue cheese, crumbled
1/2 cup crème fraîche
salt and freshly ground black pepper
12 ounces tagliatelle

1 Wash the spinach and arugula. Shake dry and remove any tough stalks. Place the spinach and arugula leaves in a large saucepan, cover with a lid, and cook for 5 minutes, until they have wilted in the heat of the pan and turned bright green.

2 Drain in a colander, pressing down well with a small plate to extract any excess liquid in the spinach and arugula.

3 Put the milk, butter, and crumbled blue cheese in a small pan and stir gently over very low heat until melted and blended. Stir in the crème fraîche and season to taste. Stir in the drained spinach and arugula.

4 Meanwhile, cook the tagliatelle in lightly salted boiling water until tender (*al dente*). Drain and toss in the blue cheese sauce.

Serves 4

Pasta al Pesto

If you are tempted to rush into the supermarket and buy a jar or carton of readymade pesto sauce for this recipe, don't! Homemade pesto, using the finest ingredients, is infinitely better, fresher, and a more vivid green than anything you can buy. If you can't get vegetarian Parmesan, use grano pedano or Pecorino instead.

1 pound pasta shapes
freshly ground black pepper
1/2 cup pine nuts
cup vegetarian Parmesan cheese

FOR THE PESTO SAUCE:
1/2 cup pine nuts

2 garlic cloves, minced
2 ounces fresh basil leaves
1/2 cup grated vegetarian Parmesan cheese
juice of 1/2 lemon
1/2 cup olive oil

1 Make the pesto sauce: spread out the pine nuts on a cookie sheet and place in a preheated oven at 425°F for about 3–4 minutes, until they are golden brown.

2 Put the pine nuts and garlic in a blender or food processor and process to a thick paste. Add the basil leaves and process for a few seconds. Add the Parmesan cheese and lemon juice, and blend again.

3 Add the olive oil through the feed tube in a thin stream, processing all the time. You will end up with a thick green sauce.

4 Cook the pasta in lightly salted boiling water until just tender (*al dente*). Drain well, sprinkle with freshly ground black pepper, and toss in the pesto sauce. Stir in the pine nuts and serve, sprinkled with Parmesan cheese.

Serves 4

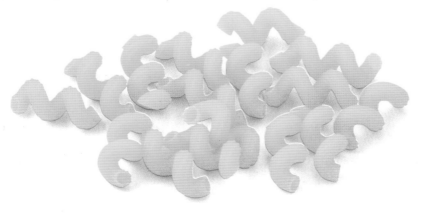

Spinach Gnocchi

To be successful, gnocchi must be light, not stodgy and rib sticking. Homemade gnocchi taste best but you can cheat and use frozen gnocchi instead. Gnocchi can be served with pesto sauce or a simple tomato sauce, or they can be baked with cheese as in this recipe.

1 Wash the spinach and remove any hard stalks. Put the leaves in a large saucepan, cover with a lid and cook gently over low heat for about 5 minutes, until the leaves wilt and turn bright green. Drain in a colander and press down with a plate to squeeze out any excess water. Chop the spinach finely.

8 ounces fresh spinach
1¼ pounds starchy potatoes, boiled
1½ cups flour
1 egg, beaten
pinch of grated nutmeg
salt and freshly ground
black pepper
6 ounces blue cheese, crumbled
⅝ cup heavy cream

2 Mash the potatoes thoroughly to remove any lumps—ideally, pass them through a food mill. Beat in the spinach, flour, egg, nutmeg, and seasoning.

3 Turn out the mixture on to a lightly floured board and knead well until

the dough is soft and pliable. Then, with floured hands, roll small pieces of dough into "sausage" shapes, the thickness of your thumb. Press down on each one with the tines of a fork.

4 Put the gnocchi into a large saucepan of lightly salted boiling water and cook rapidly until they rise to the surface and float. Remove with a slotted spoon and arrange in a buttered ovenproof dish.

5 Scatter the blue cheese over the gnocchi and pour the cream over the top. Bake in a preheated oven at 375°F for 10–15 minutes, until bubbling and golden.

Serves 4

Polenta with Sicilian Tomato Sauce

Traditionally polenta is peasant food—hearty and rustic. However, it has now become an elegant and fashionable dish, toasted or fried in good olive oil or butter. You can serve it either way in this recipe, soft or fried, with a piquant fresh tomato and chili sauce. To make soft polenta decadently rich and wonderful, stir in some mascarpone, sliced

4½ cups water
salt
1 cup polenta
2 tablespoons sweet butter
olive oil or butter for frying
(optional)
grated Parmesan cheese and fresh
basil, to serve

FOR THE TOMATO SAUCE:
3 tablespoons olive oil

1 small onion, chopped
2 garlic cloves, minced
1 red chili, seeded and finely chopped
1 pound plum tomatoes, seeded and
chopped
2 tablespoons capers, drained
2 tablespoons toasted pine nuts
1 cup black olives, pitted and
roughly chopped
few basil leaves, torn
salt and freshly ground black pepper

Taleggio, or crumbled Gorgonzola cheese before serving.

1 Make the polenta: bring the water and salt to the boil in a large saucepan. Add the polenta gradually in a thin, steady stream, beating all the time. Reduce the

heat as low as it will go and continue stirring the polenta with a wooden spoon until it is thick and smooth and has absorbed all the liquid. This takes about 15–20 minutes.

2 When the polenta leaves the sides of the pan clean, stir in the butter.

You can serve the polenta like this, all fluffed up like mashed potatoes, adding some grated cheese and black pepper, if wished, or you can pour it into an oiled pan and leave to cool. When cold, cut into squares and fry in olive oil or butter until crisp and golden.

3 To make the tomato sauce, heat the olive oil and gently cook the onion and garlic until soft. Add the chili and cook for 2 minutes. Stir in the tomatoes, capers, pine nuts, and olives and simmer gently, uncovered, for 30 minutes, until thickened. Stir in the torn basil leaves and seasoning.

Polenta with Sicilian Tomato Sauce

4 Serve the sauce with the polenta, sprinkled with some freshly grated Parmesan cheese and garnish with more basil.

Serves 4

Rice, Grains, & Legumes

Rice, grains, and legumes are all nutritious staple foods for vegetarians, being rich in protein, fiber, vitamins, and minerals. Ideally, they should form an important part of your daily diet. As well as regular long-grain rice, you will discover grain dishes using couscous and crunchy bulgur wheat. Legumes can make your diet more interesting and healthy. Try the Caribbean fritters or Mexican tacos and see for yourself.

Vegetable **Couscous**

Couscous is the fluffy grain of the Mahgreb, the countries of North Africa. Traditionally, it is steamed above a spicy bubbling stew, and red hot harissa paste is stirred into the vegetable mixture just before serving the couscous.

3 tablespoons olive oil
1 onion, chopped
2 garlic cloves, minced
1 eggplant, cut into large cubes
2 zucchini, cut into chunks
1 red bell pepper, seeded and cut into chunks
2 teaspoons ground cumin
1 teaspoon turmeric
1 teaspoon paprika
$1/2$ teaspoon ground ginger
$1/2$ teaspoon allspice

$2^1/_2$ cups passata (sieved tomatoes)
$5/8$ cup vegetable broth
1 cup canned garbanzos, drained
$1/4$ cup presoaked dried apricots, sliced
$1^1/_3$ cups couscous
2 teaspoons harissa paste
salt and freshly ground black pepper
2 tablespoons chopped fresh cilantro

1 Heat the olive oil in a deep saucepan and gently fry the onion and garlic until soft and golden. Add the eggplant, zucchini, and red bell pepper and fry gently, stirring occasionally, for 5 minutes.

2 Stir in all the spices and cook gently for 1 minute. Add the passata and the broth and bring to the boil. Reduce the heat to a simmer and stir in the garbanzo peas and apricots. Simmer for 20–25 minutes, until the vegetables are tender and the liquid has reduced.

3 About 10 minutes before serving, put the couscous in a colander lined with cheesecloth and place above the simmering vegetables.

4 Fork through the couscous to separate the grains and fluff it up. Spoon it onto the warmed serving plates. Mix the harissa paste with a little of the sauce, and either serve it separately or stir it back into the vegetable stew. Check the seasoning and serve the stew with the couscous, sprinkled with cilantro.

Serves 4

Opposite: Vegetable Couscous

Rice 'n Peas

This is a popular dish in Jamaica. The "peas" are really red kidney, pinto, or navy beans. If you are in a hurry, substitute canned beans.

1 cup dried beans
1 tablespoon peanut oil
1 onion, finely chopped
2 1/2 cups coconut milk
1 1/4 cups vegetable broth
2 sprigs of fresh thyme
bunch of scallions,
finely chopped
1 fresh red chili, seeded and finely
chopped
salt and freshly ground
black pepper
1 1/2 cups long-grain rice
chopped cilantro, to garnish

1 Put the dried beans in a saucepan, cover with cold water, and bring to the boil. Boil the beans for 10 minutes, and then remove from the heat. Set aside to soak in the cooking liquid for at least 1 hour. Drain and rinse the beans, return to the pan, and cover with fresh water. Bring back to the boil, then reduce the heat and simmer gently for about 1 hour, until tender. Drain and set aside.

2 Meanwhile, heat the peanut oil in another saucepan and fry the onion until soft and golden. Add the coconut milk, vegetable broth, thyme, scallions, and chili. Season with salt and pepper and cook over medium heat for 5 minutes.

3 Tip in the rice and stir well. Cover the pan and simmer very gently for about 20 minutes, until the rice is tender and all the liquid has been absorbed. Check occasionally to make sure that the rice is not sticking, and add more liquid if necessary.

4 Stir the cooked beans into the rice and sprinkle with cilantro. Serve with roasted or grilled vegetables and West Indian hot pepper sauce.

Serves 4

Bulgur Wheat Pilaf

In Turkey and the Middle East, bulgur wheat is often used in pilafs in preference to rice. Its crisp, chewy texture and nutty flavor make it a delicious and nourishing grain for vegetarians.

4 tablespoons fruity green
olive oil
1 onion, finely chopped
1 fresh red chili, seeded and finely
chopped
2 1/2 cups bulgur wheat
2 1/2 cups boiling vegetable broth
salt and freshly ground
black pepper
2 tablespoons chopped parsley
or cilantro

FOR THE TOPPING:
1 red bell pepper, seeded
and chopped
1 green bell pepper, seeded
and chopped
4 ounces creamy goat's cheese or
Camembert, thinly sliced

1 Heat the olive oil in a saucepan and gently fry the onion until it is soft and translucent. Add the chili and cook for 2–3 minutes.

2 Stir in the bulgur wheat and add the boiling vegetable broth. Reduce the heat and simmer for about 20 minutes, until the bulgur wheat has swelled up and absorbed the liquid. Season with salt and pepper.

3 While the pilaf is cooking, broil the bell peppers, turning occasionally, until the skin blackens all over. Peel the peppers, remove the seeds, and cut the flesh into strips.

4 Transfer the cooked pilaf to an ovenproof dish, and arrange the bell peppers and sliced cheese on top. Cook under a preheated broiler until the cheese starts to melt and turn golden. Serve sprinkled with chopped parsley or cilantro.

Serves 4

Persian Pilaf

1 cup long-grain rice
2 tablespoons oil
1 onion, finely chopped
1 teaspoon ground turmeric
1/2 teaspoon allspice
1/2 teaspoon ground cinnamon
4 green cardamom pods
2 cups vegetable broth
1/4 cup presoaked dried apricots,
coarsely chopped
salt and ground black pepper
1 tablespoon pine nuts
2 tablespoons shelled pistachios
1 tablespoon toasted slivered almonds
few cilantro leaves, torn

Many of the classic rice dishes of the Middle East and North Africa are flavored with spices and fruit. This may seem an unusual combination nowadays but they date from the Middle Ages when apricots, quinces, and dates were often included in savory dishes.

1 Place the rice in a colander and wash thoroughly under cold running water.

2 Heat the oil in a large saucepan and fry the onion until soft and golden. Stir in all the spices and cook for 2–3 minutes, until they release their aroma.

3 Stir in the rice and vegetable broth, and bring to a boil. Reduce the heat, stir in the apricots, and cover the pan. Simmer gently for 15–20 minutes, until the rice has fluffed up and absorbed the liquid.

4 Season to taste and sprinkle with the nuts before serving. If wished, scatter some torn cilantro leaves over the top.

Serves 4

Vegetable Biriyani

You don't have to go out to an Indian restaurant to enjoy a spicy vegetable biriyani. All the ingredients are now available in your local food market.

3 tablespoons ghee or vegetable oil
1 large onion, finely chopped
2 garlic cloves, minced
6 cloves
4 green cardamom pods
1-inch cinnamon stick
1 fresh green chili, finely chopped
1-inch piece fresh ginger root, peeled
and chopped
2 cups Basmati rice
2 carrots, cubed
1 small cauliflower, divided into florets
2 zucchini, sliced thickly

1/4 pound okra, trimmed and
sliced thickly
1/2 cup shelled peas
2 1/2 cups vegetable broth
2 tablespoons ground coriander seeds
1 teaspoon ground cumin
3 tablespoons golden raisins
salt and freshly ground black pepper

FOR THE GARNISH:
2 tablespoons sweet butter or ghee
2 large onions, sliced
3 tablespoons slivered almonds

1 Heat the ghee or oil in a large saucepan and fry the onion and garlic until soft and golden. Stir in the cloves, cardamom pods, cinnamon, chili, and ginger. Fry gently for 2–3 minutes.

2 Add the rice and cook over low heat, stirring occasionally, for 5 minutes, until all the grains are translucent and glistening.

3 Add the prepared vegetables and vegetable broth. Bring to a boil, then reduce the heat and add the remaining spices. Simmer gently for 25–30 minutes, until the vegetables are tender and the rice is cooked and plumped up. It should absorb all the liquid. Check the pan from time to time, adding more liquid if necessary. Stir in the golden raisins and seasoning to taste.

4 While the rice is cooking, heat the butter or ghee in a skillet and fry the onions until they are golden brown.

Remove with a slotted spoon and drain on paper towels.

5 Serve the biriyani sprinkled with the fried onions and almonds. A yogurt raita or tomato and cilantro relish makes a good accompaniment.

Serves 4

Creole **Coconut** Rice

2 tablespoons peanut oil
1 small onion, chopped
1 garlic clove, minced
2 red chilies, seeded and
finely chopped
1 cup long-grain rice
2¹/₂ cups coconut milk
salt and freshly ground
black pepper
grated rind of 1 lime
1 tablespoon chopped chives
lime wedges and sprigs of
cilantro, to garnish

This aromatic rice evokes the flavors and fragrances of the Caribbean. Serve it with grilled or curried vegetables, fried bananas, and some fiery West Indian hot pepper sauce.

1 Heat the oil in a deep skillet and gently fry the onion and garlic until golden. Add the chilies and fry for 2–3 minutes.

2 Stir in the rice and add the coconut milk. Bring to a boil, then reduce the heat and simmer very gently for 15–20 minutes, until the rice is tender and has absorbed all the liquid. Keep checking the rice while it is cooking to check that it is not sticking to the base of the skillet.

3 Cover the pan with a lid and set aside to steam gently for 5 minutes. Fluff up the rice with a fork and sprinkle with the lime rind. Season to taste, scatter the chives over the top, and serve garnished with lime wedges and sprigs of cilantro.

Serves 4

Vegetable **Paella**

This vibrant colorful dish is familiar to anyone who has visited Spain. It should be made with Spanish Valencia rice but you could use Arborio or risotto rice instead. Many regional variations exist, but rice and saffron are the two ingredients that are common to all of them. Don't leave out the saffron or use turmeric instead—there is no substitute for the real thing.

3 tablespoons fruity green
olive oil
2 onions, chopped
2 garlic cloves, minced
1 red bell pepper, seeded and
sliced in rings
1 yellow bell pepper, seeded and
sliced in rings
1 pound tomatoes, skinned
and chopped
¹/₂ pound thin green beans,
trimmed
1 pound peas in their
pods, shelled
2 cups Valencia or
Arborio rice
1 teaspoon paprika
1¹/₄ cups dry white wine
¹/₂ teaspoon saffron
3³/₄ cups boiling
vegetable broth
salt and freshly ground
black pepper
3 tablespoons chopped parsley

1 Heat the olive oil in a paella pan or a large shallow skillet. Fry the onions and garlic gently until soft and golden. Add the bell peppers and fry for 4–5 minutes. Then add the tomatoes, beans, and peas and cook for another 5 minutes.

2 Add the rice and paprika and stir well. Pour in the white wine and bring to a boil. Mix the saffron with the boiling broth and pour into the skillet. Reduce the heat a little and simmer for 5 minutes.

3 Cover the skillet with a lid or some kitchen foil and place in the bottom of a preheated oven at 350°F for 30–40 minutes, until the rice is tender and has absorbed all the broth. Alternatively, simmer on top of the stove in the same way as you would cook a risotto. Season to taste and stand, covered, for 5 minutes before serving, sprinkled with parsley.

Serves 4–6

Opposite: Vegetable Paella

Mushroom risotto

Serves 4

Risotto is one of the world's most soothing, comforting dishes. It is Italian cooking at its simplest and best. The basic ingredients that are common to all risottos are butter, Arborio rice, saffron, and homemade broth. To these you can add the vegetables of your choice to make an infinite variety of risottos: artichoke, asparagus, fresh herb, mushroom, fresh or sun-dried tomato, or even truffle risotto.

4 tablespoons butter
1 onion, finely chopped
1¹/₂ cups risotto rice
¹/₂ cup dry
white wine
1 pound exotic mushrooms,
thinly sliced
7 ¹/₂ cups vegetable broth
(see page 139)
a few threads of saffron

salt and freshly ground
black pepper

TO SERVE:
1 tablespoon butter
3 tablespoons grated vegetarian
Parmesan cheese
3 tablespoons finely chopped
parsley

3 Add the mushrooms and stir gently until they are coated with oil.

4 Add some of the boiling vegetable broth immediately with the saffron, and cook over moderate heat, stirring from time to time. Add more broth as and when it is needed—the rice should absorb it gradually. When the rice is tender and creamy and all the broth has been absorbed, remove the skillet from the heat. Season to taste and stir in the butter and Parmesan cheese. Sprinkle with parsley and serve piping hot.

1 Melt the butter in a large heavy skillet, and fry the onion until soft and golden.

2 Add the rice, stirring well with a wooden spoon until all the grains are glistening and translucent. Pour in the wine and turn up the heat. Boil rapidly until it reduces.

Lima **Beans** with Mushroom Sauce

two 14-ounce cans lima beans
2 tablespoons butter
1 small onion, chopped
12 ounces open cap mushrooms, thinly sliced
5/8 cup white wine or Madeira
1 tablespoon chopped tarragon
5/8 cup heavy cream
pinch of grated nutmeg
1 teaspoon whole grain mustard
salt and freshly ground black pepper
3/4 cup grated Cheddar cheese

This is a quick standby supper when you don't have time to cook a big meal. Eat it with crisp salad and some crusty or ciabatta bread. You can use dried beans soaked overnight and then cook them until tender, but canned beans are much more convenient and taste just as good.

1 Rinse the beans in a colander under running cold water, and drain well.

2 Melt the butter in a large skillet, add the onion and cook gently until soft and translucent. Add the mushrooms and cook for about 5 minutes, until colored.

3 Stir in the wine or Madeira and tarragon, and turn up the heat. Let it bubble until the liquid is reduced and slightly syrupy.

4 Add the cream, nutmeg, and mustard and simmer gently for 2–3 minutes. Stir in the drained lima beans, and season to taste. Sprinkle the Cheddar cheese over the top and place briefly under a preheated broiler until the cheese melts and starts to bubble. Serve with a salad.

Serves 4

Caribbean **Accras**

These little fritters, which are made with ground black-eyed peas, are eaten widely as an appetizer with rum punch throughout the Caribbean, especially in the French speaking islands. If you can get them, use the red hot Scotch bonnet chilies.

1 Put the black-eyed peas in a bowl, cover with cold water, and leave to soak overnight. The following day, drain the peas and rinse them under cold running water. Rub off the skins between your fingers.

1 1/3 cups black-eyed peas
2 fresh red chilies, seeded and chopped
1 garlic clove, minced
good pinch of salt
1–2 tablespoons milk
oil for deep-frying

2 Put the peas in a blender or food processor with the chilies, garlic, and salt and process until you have a smooth, thick paste.

3 Spoon into a bowl and beat well with a wooden spoon. Beat in enough milk to make a lighter, fluffier mixture.

4 Heat the oil to 375°F and then drop in teaspoonfuls of the mixture, a few at a time, and fry until golden brown all over. Remove with a slotted spoon, drain on paper towels and keep warm while you fry the remaining mixture in the same way. Serve hot. A bowl of salsa (see page 16) or mango relish goes well with the accras.

Serves 4

Spicy Dal

1 cup split red lentils
3³/₄ cups water
¹/₂ teaspoon ground turmeric
4 tablespoons sweet butter or ghee
1 small onion, thinly sliced
2 garlic cloves, finely chopped
1 teaspoon cumin seeds
1 teaspoon ground coriander
1 fresh green chili, seeded and
finely chopped
salt and freshly ground
black pepper
2 tablespoons chopped fresh
cilantro

Dal is a vegetarian staple in India; it can be made from red split lentils, whole green lentils, moong dal, or even dried beans. For speed and convenience, this recipe uses split red lentils, which are now readily available from food markets. Serve the dal with boiled rice or pilaf and some fresh leaf spinach and plain yogurt.

1 Put the lentils in a sieve and rinse well under running cold water. Drain and transfer to a large saucepan. Add the water and turmeric and bring to the boil. Skim any scum off the surface, then cover the pan and simmer gently for about 1-1¹/₄ hours, until the lentils are tender and slightly mushy. Stir occasionally to prevent them from sticking.

2 While the lentils are cooking, heat the butter or ghee in a skillet and fry the onion and garlic until soft and colored. Add the spices and chili and cook for 2–3 minutes, until they release their aroma.

3 Stir the spicy onion mixture into the cooked lentils, season, and serve sprinkled with cilantro. If wished, you can beat the lentil mixture with a wooden spoon until thick and puréed, stir in the onions and serve.

Serves 4

Bean Crumble

This is a variation on the cassoulets of southwest France: haricot beans in a robust red wine and tomato sauce, topped with a savory nutty crumble.

1 cup pinto or navy beans
1 onion, studded with 3 cloves
1 bay leaf
2 tablespoons olive oil
1 large onion, chopped
1 garlic clove, minced
2 carrots, sliced
2 tablespoons tomato paste
1 tablespoon chopped oregano
and parsley
¹/₂ cup red wine
4 tomatoes, skinned and chopped

1 teaspoon brown sugar
salt and freshly ground
black pepper
few drops of soy sauce

FOR THE CRUMBLE:
³/₄ cup whole-wheat flour
¹/₃ cup old-fashioned oats
salt and pepper
3 tablespoons butter, diced
2 tablespoons chopped Brazil-nuts
3 tablespoons grated cheese

1 Soak the beans in cold water overnight. Drain and refresh under cold running water. Place the beans in a saucepan with the onion and bay leaf, cover with water, and bring to a boil. Reduce the heat and simmer for 2 hours, until tender. Drain the beans, reserving ¹/₂ cup of the cooking liquid.

2 Heat the oil in a flameproof casserole dish and fry the onion, garlic, and carrots until soft. Stir in the remaining ingredients and bring to a boil. Reduce the heat and add the drained beans and reserved cooking liquid. Cover the dish and cook in a preheated oven at 350°F for 30 minutes.

3 Meanwhile, make the crumble. Put the flour, oats, and seasoning in a bowl and cut in the butter. Mix in the nuts and cheese.

4 After 30 minutes, remove the dish from the oven and sprinkle the crumble mixture over the top. Increase the oven temperature to 400°F and bake, uncovered, for a further 30–40 minutes.

Serves 4

Bean **Tacos**

Another Mexican dish. Here, the tortillas are stuffed with a spicy bean mixture and are then fried until golden and crisp. You can now buy readymade flour or corn soft tortillas in most food markets.

2 tablespoons olive oil
1 large onion, chopped
2 garlic cloves, minced
2 fresh red chilies, seeded and finely chopped
1 tablespoon tomato paste
one 14-ounce can chopped tomatoes
two 14-ounce cans navy beans or black beans
salt and freshly ground black pepper
2 tablespoons chopped fresh cilantro

12 tortillas
oil for frying

TO SERVE:
1/2 cup grated Cheddar or Monterey Jack cheese
1/2 cup sour cream
1 quantity salsa (see page 16)
guacamole (see page 141) or diced avocado

1 Heat the olive oil and fry the onion and garlic until soft and golden. Add the chilies and cook for 2-3 minutes.

2 Stir in the tomato purée and tomatoes and simmer for 10-15 minutes until the sauce reduces and thickens slightly.

3 Drain the canned beans and rinse under running cold water. Add the beans to the tomato sauce. Heat through and season to taste with salt and pepper. Stir in the coriander and remove from the heat.

4 Place a little of the tomato and bean mixture on each tortilla and roll up tightly. Secure with wooden cocktail sticks.

5 Heat the oil and fry the tacos until golden brown all over, turning occasionally. Remove and drain on paper towels. Sprinkle the hot tacos with Cheddar cheese and serve with sour cream, salsa, and guacamole.

Serves 4

Frijoles Refritos

Otherwise known as refried beans, this is the most common way of serving beans in Mexico. The beans are cooked, then fried and mashed, and the paste is used as a filling for tortillas or served hot, garnished with guacamole, sour cream, salsa, or sliced avocado.

1 cup dried pinto beans
4 garlic cloves, sliced
1 bay leaf
2 tablespoons vegetable fat or butter
1 large onion, chopped
salt and freshly ground black pepper
3/4 cup grated Cheddar or Monterey Jack cheese

1 Put the beans in a large bowl, cover with cold water and soak overnight. Drain the beans and rinse well under cold running water.

2 Put the beans, garlic cloves, and bay leaf in a large saucepan. Cover with plenty of cold water and bring to the boil. Reduce the heat and simmer gently for 2 hours, or until the beans are cooked and tender. Drain the beans, reserving the cooking liquid.

3 Put the drained beans in a large bowl and mash coarsely, adding some of the reserved cooking liquid.

4 Heat the vegetable fat or butter in a large skillet and gently fry the onion until soft and golden. Add the mashed beans, stir well, and cook over low heat for a few minutes. Add some more of the cooking liquid if necessary. Season to taste with salt and pepper.

5 Serve the refried beans very hot, sprinkled with the grated cheese.

Serves 4

Opposite: Bean Tacos

Provençal **Bean** Casserole

You need a strong bodied red wine for this country-style casserole. Serve it with baked potatoes and green vegetables for a warming winter supper.

1⅓ cups dried navy beans
2 tablespoons butter
2 tablespoons olive oil
1 onion, finely chopped
1 garlic clove, minced
2 carrots, sliced
4 tomatoes, skinned
and chopped
1¼ cups red wine
1 bouquet garni
2 sprigs of rosemary
2-inch piece of
orange rind
¾ cup black olives, pitted
salt and freshly ground
black pepper
3 tablespoons chopped
parsley or basil

1 Soak the beans in cold water overnight. Drain and rinse under cold running water. Put the beans into a large saucepan, cover with fresh water and bring to the boil. Reduce the heat and simmer for about 1 hour, until the beans are tender. Drain and set aside.

2 Heat the butter and olive oil in a heavy saucepan or flameproof casserole dish, and fry the onion, garlic, and carrots until soft. Add the tomatoes, red wine, bouquet garni, rosemary, and orange rind and bring to a boil. Cook over medium to high heat to reduce the liquid by half. Add the drained navy beans and then simmer gently for 10–15 minutes.

3 Add the olives and continue cooking gently for 5 minutes. Season to taste with salt and pepper and remove the bouquet garni and rosemary sprigs. Serve sprinkled with parsley or basil.

Serves 4

Pasta and **Beans**

1 cup dried borlotti or navy beans
1 carrot, sliced
1 onion, sliced
1 stalk celery, sliced
5 cups vegetable broth
½ pound pasta tubes or shapes
3 cups shredded green cabbage
¼ cup grated vegetarian
Parmesan cheese

FOR THE TOMATO SAUCE:
3 tablespoons olive oil
1 onion, chopped
2 garlic cloves, crushed
1¼ cups passata (sieved
tomatoes)
2 tablespoons chopped parsley
salt and freshly ground black pepper

This wonderful dish of borlotti beans and pasta can be eaten as a hearty soup or, as served in Italy, as a main course with plenty of crusty bread to mop up the juices.

1 Soak the beans in cold water overnight. Drain and place in a large saucepan with the carrot, onion, celery stalk, and broth. Bring to the boil, then reduce the heat and simmer for about 1 hour, until the beans are cooked and tender.

2 Meanwhile, make the tomato sauce. Heat the olive oil and fry the onion and garlic until soft and golden. Stir in the passata and simmer for 15–20 minutes, until thickened. Add the parsley and season to taste.

3 Remove a large ladle of beans from the pan, and purée them in a blender or food processor. Return to the other beans in the cooking liquid, and stir in the tomato sauce and pasta.

4 Simmer for 10–15 minutes, until the pasta is tender. About 5 minutes before serving, stir in the shredded green cabbage. Check the seasoning and serve in large deep plates or bowls, sprinkled with freshly grated Parmesan cheese.

Serves 6

Mexican **Bean** Stew

1¹/₃ cups dried
navy or black beans
3 tablespoons vegetable oil
2 onions, chopped
1 garlic clove, minced
2 small fresh red chilies, seeded
and finely chopped
1¹/₄ pounds pumpkin
2 fresh ears of corn
two 14-ounce cans
chopped tomatoes
salt and freshly ground
black pepper
2 tablespoons chopped
fresh cilantro
sour cream and diced avocado, for
the topping

Beans are combined with corn and pumpkin in this fiery stew. You can use almost any dried beans—red kidney, navy, black, lima, or borlotti beans are all suitable. Remember, when cooking beans never to add salt to the cooking water, as this will harden the beans. Always season them after cooking.

1 Put the dried navy or black beans in a bowl, cover with cold water and leave to soak for several hours or overnight. The following day, drain and rinse them under cold running water. Tip the beans into a large saucepan, cover with fresh water and bring to the boil. Lower the heat and simmer for about 1 hour, until the beans are cooked and

tender. Drain well, reserving the cooking liquid.

2 Heat the oil and fry the onions and garlic until soft and golden. Add the chilies and fry for 2–3 minutes.

3 Remove the rind and seeds from the pumpkin and cut the flesh into chunks. Remove the kernels from the corn. Add the pumpkin and corn to the pan with the tomatoes and drained beans. Simmer gently for 20–30 minutes, adding some of the reserved cooking liquid from the beans if necessary. Season to taste.

4 Serve the Mexican Bean Stew hot, sprinkled with cilantro and topped with a spoonful of sour cream and some diced avocado.

Serves 4

Creamy **Flageolet** Beans

Pale green flageolets are the most elegant and delicate of all the dried beans. If you don't have time to cook, you can use canned ones instead. If you can't get flageolets, substitute navy or lima beans.

1¹/₃ cups dried flageolet
beans
2 tablespoons butter
1 onion, finely chopped
2 garlic cloves, minced
few sprigs of tarragon,
chopped
⁵/₈ cup light cream or crème
fraîche
1 teaspoon Dijon mustard
salt and freshly ground black pepper
fresh tarragon leaves,
to garnish

1 Soak the beans in cold water overnight. The following day, drain and rinse under running cold water. Place in a large saucepan, cover with cold water, and bring to a boil. Reduce the heat and simmer until the beans are tender. Drain well.

2 Melt the butter in a skillet and gently fry the onion and garlic until soft and golden. Add the chopped tarragon and stir into the onion mixture with the drained beans.

3 Add the cream and Dijon mustard and turn up the heat. Just before it boils, reduce the heat and simmer for 2–3 minutes. Season to taste and serve immediately, sprinkled with tarragon leaves.

Serves 4

Eggs & Cheese

Eggs and cheese have a natural affinity and are an important source of protein for most vegetarians. Most cheeses are produced using animal rennet, but you can buy vegetarian alternatives, which are made with microbial enzymes. These are now stocked by many food markets. Always opt for free-range eggs rather than battery or factory farmed ones.

Egg-fried **Noodles**

Egg noodles stir-fried with colorful fresh vegetables and eggs make a meal in minutes. Almost any vegetables are suitable for this dish; other suggestions include mushrooms; sliced scallions; red, orange, and green bell peppers; eggplant; baby corn; snow peas; green beans; and little cauliflower florets.

8 ounces dried egg noodles
1/2 pound broccoli florets
1/4 pound thin asparagus, trimmed and sliced
4 tablespoons corn oil
2 garlic cloves, sliced
1 small onion, chopped
1-inch piece fresh ginger root, chopped
1 fresh red chili, seeded and finely chopped
1 small yellow bell pepper, seeded and thinly sliced
grated rind and juice of 1/2 lime
1 tablespoon yellow bean paste
1 teaspoon sugar
2 eggs
salt and freshly ground black pepper
2 tablespoons chopped fresh cilantro
dark soy sauce, to serve

1 Bring a large saucepan of water to a boil and plunge the egg noodles into the boiling water. Cook for a few minutes until tender. Drain and rinse in a colander under running cold water to prevent the noodles sticking together.

2 Cook the broccoli and the asparagus in a pan of boiling water for 2–3 minutes. Drain well.

3 Heat the vegetable oil in a wok and fry the garlic, onion, ginger, and chili for 1–2 minutes over high heat. Add the yellow bell pepper and the blanched broccoli and asparagus. Stir-fry for 1 minute, then add the lime rind and juice, yellow bean paste, and sugar.

4 Stir in the drained noodles and break the eggs into the wok. Stir gently for 1–2 minutes, until they are soft and only just set. Season to taste with salt and pepper, then sprinkle the chopped fresh cilantro over the noodle mixture and serve immediately. Serve the dark soy sauce separately.

Serves 4

Opposite: Egg-fried Noodles

Huevos Rancheros

This is a Mexican way of cooking eggs. As you would expect, hot chilies and tomatoes feature strongly in the recipe.

2 tablespoons oil
1 large onion, finely chopped
2 garlic cloves, minced
1 red bell pepper, seeded and chopped
2 fresh green chilies, seeded and finely chopped
4 large tomatoes, seeded and chopped
2 tablespoons tomato paste
$1/2$ cup vegetable broth
pinch of sugar
salt and freshly ground black pepper
4 eggs
2 tablespoons chopped fresh cilantro
1 large avocado, pitted, peeled, and sliced

1 Heat the oil in a saucepan and fry the onion, garlic, red bell pepper, and chilies until soft.

2 Add the tomatoes, tomato paste, vegetable broth, and sugar. Bring to a boil, then reduce the heat and simmer gently until the sauce reduces and thickens slightly. Season to taste with salt and pepper.

3 Pour the tomato sauce into an oiled ovenproof dish. Make 4 hollows in the sauce with the back of a spoon, and break the eggs into them.

4 Bake in a preheated oven at 350°F for 10–12 minutes, until the eggs are set and cooked. Serve sprinkled with chopped cilantro and garnish with sliced avocado.

Serves 4

Vegetable Frittata

This aromatic Italian omelet is packed with vegetables and finished off under a hot broiler. It is best served warm or at room temperature, cut into wedges, with a dressed salad. As well as making a good light lunch or supper dish, it is the ideal finger food for summer picnics.

3 tablespoons olive oil
2 onions, thinly sliced
3 zucchini, thinly sliced
3 tomatoes, skinned and chopped
6 large eggs
salt and freshly ground black pepper
$1/2$ cup grated pecorino cheese
few fresh basil leaves, chopped
2 tablespoons chopped fresh parsley
2 tablespoons butter
grated vegetarian Parmesan cheese, to serve

1 Heat the olive oil in a large skillet, and gently fry the onions for 8–10 minutes, until softened, golden brown, and almost caramelized.

2 Add the zucchini and cook for a few minutes, until golden on both sides, stirring occasionally. Stir in the tomatoes and cook over moderate heat for 8–10 minutes, until the mixture is reduced and thickened.

3 Break the eggs into a large bowl with the seasoning, grated cheese, and herbs. Beat with a whisk until well blended. Stir the tomato mixture into the beaten eggs and mix gently.

4 Melt the butter in a clean skillet and, when it is sizzling, pour in the omelet mixture. Reduce the heat to the barest simmer and cook the omelet until it is set and golden underneath.

5 Sprinkle with Parmesan cheese and place the skillet under a preheated broiler to brown the top of the omelet. Slide out onto a serving plate and serve at room temperature.

Serves 4

Stuffed **Crêpes**

1 cup all-purpose flour
pinch of salt
2 eggs
1¼ cups milk
butter for frying
filling of your choice
(see below)
¾ cup grated Swiss cheese

Lacy, thin crêpes, filled with a savory mixture of vegetables and cheese, are a specialty of Brittany, France. Here is a basic recipe for the crêpes, together with lots of ideas for fillings.

1 Sift the flour and salt into a bowl and make a hollow in the center. Break in the eggs and a little of the milk. Beat well to make a thick batter, then gradually beat in the remaining milk until the batter is smooth. Alternatively, you can make the batter in a food processor. Let the batter stand for at least 30 minutes before making the crêpes.

2 Melt a small amount of butter in a small skillet, and when it is hot and sizzling pour in 2–3 tablespoons of batter—enough to coat the base of the skillet. Tilt the skillet to distribute the batter evenly. Cook for 1–2 minutes, until the underside of the crêpe is set and golden, then turn it over and cook the other side. Slide it out onto a warm plate, then cook the remaining crêpes in the same way.

3 Fill the crêpes with the filling of your choice and roll them up into cylinder shapes or fold over. Arrange in an ovenproof dish and sprinkle the grated cheese over the top. Bake in a preheated oven at 350°F for 8–10 minutes, until the cheese is golden brown and bubbling.

Serves 4

Fillings for crêpes

1 Sliced mushrooms sautéed in butter, then mixed with a little crème fraîche and chopped chervil and chives.

2 Sliced red and yellow bell peppers stewed in olive oil with oregano or marjoram.

3 Ratatouille of eggplants, bell peppers, zucchini, and tomatoes.

4 Cooked leaf spinach mixed with diced gorgonzola or blue cheese.

5 Grilled tomatoes with goat's cheese or mozzarella.

6 Peas and asparagus in a creamy tarragon and chervil sauce.

7 Spinach and ricotta filling flavored with nutmeg

8 Sliced camembert or brie and fresh cranberry sauce.

9 Caramelized onions "stewed" in butter and white wine with plenty of chopped fresh herbs.

10 Fromage frais mixed with chopped tomato, avocado, scallions, and parsley.

11 Wilted arugula, cooked in olive oil, with sliced goat's cheese.

12 Creamy blue cheese, sliced apple, and toasted walnuts.

Quick **Welsh Rabbit**

4 slices bread, toasted
2 heaped tablespoons
fruity chutney or relish
2 cups grated Cheddar cheese
1 tablespoon mustard
2 tablespoons butter, softened
2–3 tablespoons beer
few drops of Worcestershire sauce

You can use virtually any cheese, but the strongly flavored hard ones are best, such as a mature Cheddar or Monterey Jack.

1 Spread the toast with the chutney. Mix the grated cheese with the mustard and butter and then stir in the beer and a few drops of Worcestershire sauce. Spread over the top of the chutney.

2 Put the slices of toast under a preheated hot broiler, and cook until they are golden brown and bubbling. Eat immediately as a snack.

Serves 4

Green vegetable soufflé

Serves 4

A soufflé is always a spectacular creation that inspires admiration. Instead of making a mundane cheese soufflé, why not try this light-as-air vegetable soufflé, flecked with green spinach, zucchini, and broccoli? Other puréed vegetables, such as onions, asparagus, cauliflower, parsnips, or even cabbage, are also suitable. Experiment with different cheeses—vegetarian Parmesan, Cheddar, Swiss, and even crumbled goat's cheese—to vary the flavor.

1 pound fresh spinach, zucchini, and broccoli	4 large eggs, separated, plus 1 egg white
3 tablespoons butter	$^{1}/_{2}$ cup grated Swiss cheese
3 tablespoons flour	salt and freshly ground black pepper
$^{5}/_{8}$ cup hot milk	2 tablespoons finely grated vegetarian Parmesan cheese
$^{1}/_{2}$ teaspoon grated nutmeg	

1 Wash the fresh spinach leaves thoroughly and remove any hard stalks. Trim the zucchini and slice them. Trim the stalks of the broccoli. Put all the prepared vegetables into a large saucepan of boiling lightly salted water and cook until tender. Drain well and then purée in a food processor.

2 Melt the butter in a saucepan and stir in the flour. Cook for 1 minute without coloring, and then beat in the hot milk, a little at a time, until thick, glossy, and smooth. Remove the pan

from the heat and stir in the nutmeg. Beat in the egg yolks, one at a time, and then stir in the puréed vegetables and Swiss cheese. Season with plenty of salt and pepper.

3 Beat the egg whites in a clean, dry bowl with a clean whisk, until they are glossy and stand up in stiff peaks when you lift out the whisk. Beat one tablespoonful of the beaten egg whites into the cheese and vegetable mixture, then fold in the remaining egg whites gently with a metal spoon. Don't get carried away and start mixing or beating—just fold in a

gentle figure-eight lifting and turning movement. It does not matter if you can still see the egg white and it doesn't look uniformly green.

4 Butter a $2^{1}/_{2}$-pint soufflé dish generously and sprinkle the base and around the sides with a little of the grated Parmesan cheese. Pour the soufflé mixture into the dish and then sprinkle with the remaining Parmesan. Stand the dish on a hot cookie sheet and bake in a preheated oven at 375°F for about 30 minutes, until well-risen and golden brown on top. The crust should move only slightly; if it wobbles, return the soufflé to the oven for a few more minutes. Do not open the oven door for at least 20 minutes to check on it. And be careful not to overcook it. Serve immediately.

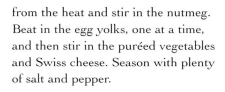

Italian **Taleggio** Pie

This is immensely rich, but a little goes a long way and it is heaven when served with a lightly dressed salad of bitter chicory, radicchio, curly endive, and arugula. If you can't find any Taleggio, use Brie, Camembert, or even a creamy goat's cheese.

1 Roll out the pastry thinly on a lightly floured surface. Cut out 2 large squares, 2 inches bigger than the piece of Taleggio.

12 ounces puff pastry, fresh or frozen and thawed
1 pound square piece of Taleggio with rind left on
beaten egg, for glazing

2 Place the cheese on top of one square, and brush the edges with beaten egg. Cover with the remaining sheet of pastry and seal and decorate the edges. Place on a greased cookie sheet, cut a small hole in the top, and brush with beaten egg. If wished, you can decorate the pie with "leaves" made from the leftover pastry.

3 If you have time, chill the pie for 15–20 minutes before baking. Bake in a preheated hot oven at 400°F for 15–20 minutes, until the pastry is well risen and golden. Resist the temptation to eat the pie immediately and let it cool a little—just 5–10 minutes—before serving with a crisp salad.

Serves 4

Gougère Puff

You rarely encounter this puffed-up savory dish outside of France, but it's well worth making. Basically, it's just a cheesey choux pastry, and it is usually served with a cocktail before the meal. However, if you bake it in a ring and then fill the center with a vegetable filling of your choice, it makes a good main course. Gougère is usually made with Gruyère, but any Swiss cheese, a mature Cheddar, or even a blue-veined cheese like Roquefort are equally delicious.

1 Put the butter and water in a saucepan and bring to a full, rolling boil. Add the flour immediately and remove the pan from the heat. Beat vigorously with a wooden spoon until the mixture forms a ball and leaves the sides of the pan clean.

³/₄ stick sweet butter
2 cups water
1 cup all-purpose flour, sifted
3 large eggs, beaten
1 cup grated Gruyère cheese
salt and freshly ground black pepper
pinch of cayenne pepper

2 Add the beaten eggs, a little at a time, beating well between each addition. You should end up with a glossy paste. Beat in three-quarters of the cheese, and season the mixture with salt, pepper, and cayenne.

3 Drop tablespoonfuls of the cheese mixture in a circle, but not quite touching, onto a well-buttered cookie tray. Sprinkle with the remaining grated Gruyère cheese.

4 Bake in a preheated oven at 425°F for 25–30 minutes, until puffed up, crisp, and golden brown. Cool for a few minutes before serving with drinks or a salad. Alternatively, spoon one of the suggested fillings listed below into the center of the cooked cheese ring.

Serves 4

Fillings

1 Ratatouille flavored with fresh herbs, e.g., oregano, basil, and parsley.

2 Sautéed mushrooms in a creamy white wine sauce.

3 Lima beans in a cream sauce flavored with whole-grain mustard and tarragon.

4 A hot salad of grilled bell peppers, avocado, and mozzarella tossed in garlic-scented olive oil.

5 Pumpkin, corn kernels, and red onions in a fresh tomato sauce.

Scrambled **Egg** Supper

When you're in a hurry and in need of comfort food, nothing beats creamy scrambled eggs. These are flavored with chives and little pockets of cream cheese.

1 Break the eggs into a bowl and beat with a fork. Stir in the chives and some salt and pepper.

2 Melt the butter in a large nonstick skillet over moderate heat. Pour in the egg mixture, then reduce the heat to a simmer and stir with a wooden spoon until the eggs are creamy and almost set.

3 Gently fold in the chilled cubes of

8 large eggs
2 tablespoons chopped chives
salt and freshly ground black pepper
3 tablespoons butter
1⅓ cups chilled cream cheese, diced
4 English muffins

cream cheese, taking care not to break them. Stir gently for 1 minute, until the eggs are set.

4 Meanwhile, split and toast the muffins. Serve the scrambled eggs piled onto the muffins.

Serves 4

Flavorings
. . . .

You can add any of the following flavorings to scrambled eggs:
. . . .

1 Diced fried mushrooms and finely chopped parsley.
. . . .

2 Chopped watercress and whole-grain mustard.
. . . .

3 Finely chopped red chilies and chopped fresh cilantro leaves.
. . . .

4 Diced tomato and chopped basil leaves.
. . . .

5 Grated cheese and chopped fresh tarragon.
. . . .

Glamorgan Cheese **Sausages**

3 cups fresh white bread crumbs
1 cup grated Cheddar cheese
3 scallions, finely chopped
1 teaspoon dried mixed herbs
2 tablespoons finely chopped parsley
good pinch of nutmeg
salt and freshly ground black pepper
1 large egg, beaten

FOR COATING AND FRYING:
1 egg white, lightly beaten
3–4 tablespoons flour
pinch of mustard powder
2 tablespoons grated vegetarian Parmesan cheese
oil for shallow frying

These delicious vegetarian "sausages" can be made with almost any cheese, but a salty Caerphilly is best if you can get it. Serve them with apple herb jelly and a mustardy watercress salad with sliced apple and walnuts.

1 Put the bread crumbs, grated cheese, scallions, herbs, and nutmeg in a bowl and mix well together. Season with salt and pepper and then stir in the beaten egg to bind the mixture together. If it is still very stiff or a little dry, moisten with a little milk.

2 Divide the mixture into 8 or 12 portions and roll each one up between your hands into a "sausage" shape.

3 Dip the "sausages" in the beaten egg white and then roll them in the flour, mustard powder, and Parmesan cheese.

4 Heat the oil in a skillet and fry the "sausages" over moderate heat, turning occasionally, until they are uniformly golden brown. Remove and drain on paper towels, then serve hot with salad.

Serves 4

Red-hot **Quesadillas**

12 fresh corn or wheat tortillas
6 ounces refried beans
(see page 50)
2 cups grated Cheddar or
Monterey Jack cheese
4 ounces Mozzarella cheese, diced
2 fresh green chilies, seeded
and finely chopped
1 tablespoon finely chopped
fresh cilantro
oil for frying

TO SERVE:
sea salt, salsa, guacamole, sour
cream, and lime wedges

Fried tortilla parcels oozing with melted cheese are now widely eaten throughout Mexico and the United States as a snack or first course. Serve with bowls of salsa, guacamole, and sour cream.

1 Spread out the tortillas and place a spoonful of refried beans on each one. Cover with grated cheese and diced Mozzarella, and scatter the chilies and cilantro over the top.

2 Dampen the edges of the tortillas and fold them over to cover the filling. Press the edges together firmly between your fingers and thumb. To be on the safe side, you can secure the tortillas with wooden toothpicks to prevent them bursting open during cooking.

3 Heat the oil in a large skillet—it should be about 1 inch deep. Fry the quesadillas, a few at a time, until they are golden brown on both sides. Remove and drain on paper towels. Serve hot sprinkled with sea salt, with salsa, guacamole, sour cream, and wedges of fresh lime.

Serves 4

Savory **Cheese** Strudel

This is an unusual savory version of the more familiar sweet strudel. Vegetable and cheese strudels are eaten in Eastern Europe, served with sour cream and sprinkled with paprika or caraway seeds.

2 tablespoons butter
2 tablespoons olive oil
1/2 pound slim leeks, washed,
trimmed, and sliced
1 1/4 cups sliced mushrooms
3 cups shredded cabbage
1 apple, peeled, cored,
and sliced
1 tablespoon cider vinegar
5 tablespoons dry cider
10 ounces creamy goat's
cheese, diced
5/8 cup sour cream
2 tablespoons chopped parsley
salt and freshly ground black pepper
6 sheets of filo pastry
6 tablespoons butter, melted

1 Heat the butter and olive oil in a large saucepan and fry the leeks until golden brown. Add the mushrooms and fry gently for 4–5 minutes, until golden. Stir in the cabbage and apple and cook gently over low heat for 2–3 minutes, until tender. Remove from the pan and keep warm.

2 Pour the cider vinegar and cider into the pan, stir well to loosen any residue from the base of the pan, and turn up the heat. Bubble rapidly until the liquid reduces and starts to get syrupy. Stir in the goat's cheese and sour cream and lower the heat to a simmer. Cook gently for 2–3 minutes, until the cheese melts into the cream, and then stir in the cooked vegetables, parsley, and seasoning.

3 Spread out 2 sheets of filo pastry, overlapping each other slightly to make a larger sheet, and brush with plenty of melted butter. Cover with half of the vegetable mixture. Cover with 2 more sheets of filo pastry, brush with more butter, and then spoon over the remaining vegetable mixture. Top with the last 2 filo sheets and brush with butter.

4 Carefully roll the pastry over lengthwise to form a cylinder. Seal the ends as best you can, and place the strudel on a buttered cookie sheet. Brush with any remaining melted butter and bake in a preheated oven at 375°F for 20–30 minutes, until the pastry is crisp and golden brown. Serve the strudel sliced with salad.

Serves 4

Opposite: Red-hot Quesadillas

Main Vegetable Dishes

In the following pages, you will find some new, innovative vegetable dishes as well as some old favorites, such as nut roast and moussaka, which have been enhanced with aromatic spices and elegant sauces to make them even more delicious. This is a truly international section featuring some of the world's best-loved vegetarian food.

Mediterranean Vegetable **Kebabs**

These kebabs can be cooked under a hot broiler or over hot coals. The vegetables are threaded on to skewers with cubes of halloumi cheese. This is ideal for grilling because it is very firm and does not ooze under the broiler.

2 eggplants, cut into large cubes
1 red bell pepper, seeded and cut into squares
1 yellow bell pepper, seeded and cut into squares
3 zucchini, cut into thick slices
3 small red onions, cut into quarters
1 pound halloumi cheese, cubed
2 tablespoons finely chopped parsley

FOR THE MARINADE:
6 tablespoons fruity green olive oil
1 garlic clove, minced
juice of 1 lemon
1 fresh red chili, seeded and chopped (optional)
salt and freshly ground black pepper

1 Prepare all the vegetables and place them in a large dish with the cubed halloumi cheese.

2 Mix the marinade ingredients together and then pour over the vegetables and cheese, turning them gently in the marinade. Cover and leave in a cool place for several hours, or overnight if wished.

3 Thread the vegetables and cheese alternately on to 4 long kebab skewers. Cook under a preheated hot broiler or over hot coals, turning occasionally, for 6–8 minutes. The vegetables should still be juicy and only slightly charred—not burnt offerings. While they are cooking, brush them frequently with the marinade to keep them moist.

4 Serve the kebabs, sprinkled with chopped parsley, with some plain boiled rice or pilaf, and a crisp salad. Salsa (see page 16) or vegetable purées (e.g., carrot or fresh pea) are also good with these kebabs.

Serves 4

Opposite: Mediterranean Vegetable Kebabs

Vegetable **Moussaka**

In some parts of Greece, moussaka is made with zucchini as well as eggplants. In this version, they are layered with black-eyed peas in tomato sauce and a white sauce, then served with pita bread.

2 eggplants, sliced
1 pound zucchini, sliced lengthwise
4 tablespoons olive oil
1 tablespoon butter
1/4 cup grated Swiss or vegetarian Parmesan cheese

FOR THE FRESH
TOMATO SAUCE:
2/3 cup black-eyed peas
2 tablespoons olive oil
2 onions, chopped
1 garlic clove, minced
one 14-ounce can chopped tomatoes
5/8 cup white wine
1 teaspoon oregano
pinch each of ground cinnamon and allspice
1 tablespoon chopped parsley
salt and freshly ground black pepper

FOR THE WHITE SAUCE:
3 tablespoons butter
3 tablespoons flour
2 cups milk
salt and freshly ground black pepper
2 egg yolks
1/4 cup grated Swiss or vegetarian Parmesan cheese

1 Prepare the black-eyed peas for the fresh tomato sauce. Soak the black-eyed peas in cold water for 1 hour. Drain well. Place in a pan, cover with fresh water, and cook for 30 minutes, until tender. Drain.

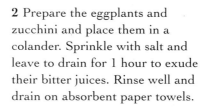

2 Prepare the eggplants and zucchini and place them in a colander. Sprinkle with salt and leave to drain for 1 hour to exude their bitter juices. Rinse well and drain on absorbent paper towels.

3 Meanwhile, heat the oil for the sauce in a saucepan and fry the onions and garlic until soft and golden. Add the tomatoes, wine, oregano, and spices, and bring to the boil. Reduce the heat and simmer for 15–20 minutes, until reduced and thickened. Stir in the cooked peas and parsley, and season to taste.

4 While the sauce is cooking, fry the eggplants and zucchini in the olive oil and butter until they are golden on both sides. Drain well on absorbent paper towels.

5 Make the white sauce: melt the butter over low heat and stir in the flour. Cook for 1 minute without coloring, then gradually add the milk, a little at a time, beating well after each addition, until the sauce is thick and smooth. Remove from the heat, season to taste, and stir in the egg yolks and grated cheese.

6 Now it's time to assemble the moussaka. Arrange a layer of eggplants and zucchini in the base of an ovenproof dish. Cover with a layer of fresh tomato sauce. Continue layering in this way, finishing with a layer of vegetables. Pour the thick white sauce over the top and then sprinkle with grated cheese.

7 Bake the moussaka in a preheated oven at 350°F for 1 hour. Remove from the oven and let stand for 5 minutes before serving.

Serves 4

Vegetable **Tempura**

1¾ pounds mixed vegetables, e.g.,
broccoli florets; zucchini batons;
button mushrooms; sliced red,
green, and yellow bell peppers;
trimmed scallions,
baby corn
oil for deep-frying
lemon wedges, to garnish
dark soy sauce

FOR THE BATTER:
1 large egg
1 cup chilled water
1¼ cups all-purpose flour
½ teaspoon salt

In Japan, vegetables are deep-fried in the lightest of batters until crisp and golden. Don't worry if some of the batter disappears into the oil. Some will end up clinging to the vegetables and the little fritters will look all the more colorful for it.

1 Make the batter. It is important to use chilled water and an egg straight from the refrigerator. Put the egg and water in a bowl with the flour and salt. Beat quickly together—do not over-beat the batter.

2 Dip the vegetables into the batter and then deep-fry, a few at a time, in oil heated to 375°F until they are crisp and golden all over. Remove the vegetables carefully with a slotted spoon and drain on absorbent paper towels. Fry the remaining vegetables in the same way.

3 Serve the vegetables with plain rice, garnished with lemon wedges. If wished, you can sprinkle a little soy sauce over them.

Serves 4

Pumpkin Curry

Make this curry in the autumn when fresh pumpkins are plentiful. In St Lucia it is served with rice, fried plantains, and the ubiquitous hot pepper sauce. However, exotic fruit salsa (see page 140) also makes a very good accompaniment. If you can't get a fresh coconut, you could use coconut milk instead.

1¼ cups grated fresh coconut,
1¼ cups coconut water (from a fresh coconut)
2 tablespoons vegetable oil
1 large onion, chopped
1 green bell pepper, seeded and chopped
4 garlic cloves, minced
1-inch piece fresh ginger root, peeled and chopped
2 fresh green chilies, seeded and finely chopped
1 tablespoon turmeric
¼ teaspoon ground cloves
2 pounds pumpkin, peeled, seeded, and diced
2 tomatoes, skinned and chopped
salt and freshly ground black pepper
fresh cilantro leaves, to garnish

1 Put the grated fresh coconut in a bowl. To get the coconut water, pierce a fresh coconut with a skewer and drain out the liquid through the hole. Pour over the grated coconut and set aside for 30 minutes.

2 Heat the oil and gently fry the onion, green bell pepper, and garlic over low heat until the onion is soft and golden brown. Stir in the ginger, chilies, turmeric, and cloves, and cook for 2–3 minutes so that the spices release their aroma.

3 Add the pumpkin, tomatoes, and coconut water. Bring to the boil, then reduce the heat and simmer for 20 minutes. The curry is ready when the pumpkin is tender and just starting to disintegrate—it should not be allowed to over-cook and go mushy. Season to taste and garnish with cilantro leaves.

4 Serve the curry immediately with boiled rice. In the West Indies, some local hot pepper sauce would be stirred into the pumpkin mixture to make it even hotter. You can buy this in most food markets.

Serves 4

Vegetable **Korma**

Serve this creamy curry with naan bread or boiled rice scattered with cardamoms and golden-brown fried onions. Mango chutney and banana raita would add the finishing touches to a delicately spicy meal.

4 tablespoons sweet butter (or ghee)
2 onions, sliced
2 garlic cloves, minced
1 fresh red chili, seeded and chopped
1-inch piece fresh ginger root, peeled and chopped
1 teaspoon turmeric
3 potatoes, peeled and cubed
1/4 pound button mushrooms
1 large eggplant, cubed
1/4 pound cauliflower florets
1 1/4 cups water or vegetable broth
1/4 pound broccoli florets

5/8 cup heavy cream
5/8 cup plain yogurt
salt and freshly ground black pepper
2 tablespoons chopped cilantro leaves
1/2 cup roasted cashews

FOR THE GROUND SPICES:
2 tablespoons coriander seeds
2 tablespoons cumin seeds
1 tablespoon cardamom seeds (from green pods)
1 teaspoon mustard seeds
6 whole cloves

1 Grind the whole spices in the traditional way with a pestle and mortar, or in an electric grinder.

2 Heat the butter (or ghee) in a deep saucepan and fry the onions and garlic until soft and golden. Add the chili and ginger and continue cooking over low heat for 2–3 minutes.

3 Stir in the ground spices and turmeric, and cook for 2 minutes. Then add the potatoes, mushrooms, eggplant, and cauliflower. Turn quickly in the spicy mixture and then pour in the water or broth. Cover the pan and simmer gently for

15–20 minutes, until the vegetables are cooked and just tender.

4 Cook the broccoli separately in boiling salted water until just tender and still bright green. Stir into the pan with the cream and yogurt and cook very gently without boiling for 4–5 minutes. The korma

will curdle if you allow it to boil!

5 Check the seasoning, adding salt and pepper to taste if needed. Serve the korma immediately, sprinkled with chopped cilantro and whole roasted cashews.

Serves 4

Vegetable **Fajitas**

This is the ideal quick supper when you are in a hurry with little time to cook. Keep a packet of tortillas in the freezer for such occasions.

2 onions, thinly sliced
1 garlic clove, minced
2 tablespoons olive oil
2 red bell peppers, seeded and sliced
1 green bell pepper, seeded and sliced
1 yellow bell pepper, seeded and sliced
2 fresh red chilies, seeded and chopped
2 1/2 cups sliced button mushrooms

salt and freshly ground black pepper
2 tablespoons finely chopped cilantro

FOR SERVING:
12 warmed tortillas
salsa (see page 16), sour cream, and guacamole
sprigs of fresh cilantro

1 Fry the onions and garlic in the olive oil until soft and golden brown. Add the bell peppers and chilies, and continue cooking until tender.

2 Add the mushrooms, turn up the heat and cook for 1 minute. Season with salt and pepper and sprinkle with chopped cilantro.

3 Put a large spoonful of the sizzling vegetables on each warmed tortilla and then roll up. Serve the fajitas immediately with bowls of salsa, sour cream, and guacamole, garnished with sprigs of fresh cilantro.

Serves: 4

Opposite: Vegetable Fajitas

Mushroom Stroganov

2 tablespoons butter
1 onion, finely chopped
1 pound mushrooms, sliced
1–2 tablespoons brandy
1 1/4 cups sour cream
pinch each of ground nutmeg
and mace
salt and ground black pepper
2 tablespoons chopped chives

FOR THE PASTA:
12 ounces tagliatelle or fettuccine
1 tablespoon melted butter
1 teaspoon caraway or
poppy seeds

Mushrooms are delicious served this way in a sour cream sauce with buttered pasta. Although button mushrooms will do, white ones are better, and shiitake mushrooms will be truly special.

1 Melt the butter in a large skillet and sauté the onion until soft and faintly golden. Add the mushrooms and fry for 4–5 minutes, until colored.

2 Stir in the brandy and let it bubble up for a few minutes until the liquid in the skillet evaporates. Stir in the sour cream and spices, and simmer gently for 5 minutes, until the sauce thickens slightly. Season to taste with salt and plenty of black pepper.

3 Meanwhile, cook the pasta in lightly salted boiling water until tender. Drain well, return to the pan and toss in the melted butter and caraway or poppy seeds.

4 Sprinkle the mushroom stroganov with chives, and serve immediately with the buttered pasta and a crisp green salad.

Serves 4

Vegetable Satay

You can make a wonderful satay with grilled spicy vegetables threaded onto small wooden skewers. Serve it with cubes of lontong rice. To make this, cook boil-in-the-bag rice for about 1 hour and then leave to cool until the rice goes solid. Remove from the bag and cut into cubes. Reheat the rice cubes before serving.

2 eggplants, cut into chunks
2 small onions, cut into chunks
1/2 pound button mushrooms
2 green bell peppers, seeded and cut
into chunks
1 yellow bell pepper, seeded and
cut into chunks
rice and cucumber
chunks, to serve
cilantro leaves, to garnish

FOR THE MARINADE:
2 garlic cloves, minced
1 tablespoon sesame oil

3 tablespoons soy sauce
1/2 teaspoon each ground ginger
and coriander
1 tablespoon lime juice
1 teaspoon brown sugar

FOR THE SATAY SAUCE:
1/2 cup roasted unsalted peanuts
1/2 teaspoon salt
1 1/4 cups coconut milk
1–2 teaspoons curry paste
1 tablespoon brown sugar
juice of 1/2 lime
good pinch of chili powder

1 Prepare the eggplants, onions, mushrooms, and bell peppers, and place in a bowl. Mix all the marinade ingredients together and spoon over the vegetables. Leave to marinate in a cool place for at least 1 hour.

2 Meanwhile, make the satay sauce. Using a pestle and mortar, grind the peanuts and salt to a thick, creamy consistency. Pour half of the coconut milk into a saucepan, stir in the curry paste, and stir over low heat

for 2–3 minutes. Add the creamed peanut mixture, sugar, lime juice, chili powder, and remaining coconut milk. Stir and then simmer for about 15–20 minutes, until thickened.

3 Thread the marinated vegetables onto oiled wooden or bamboo skewers, and cook under a hot broiler or over hot coals, turning frequently, for 6–8 minutes, until tender and ever so slightly charred. Brush them occasionally with the marinade to keep them moist.

4 Serve the vegetable skewers immediately with the satay dipping sauce, with either boiled or lontong rice and chunks of fresh cucumber. Garnish with fresh cilantro leaves.

Serves 4

Sesame Crêpes

You can prepare the crêpes in advance and reheat them later just before serving. You don't have to stick to the stir-fried vegetables in the recipe. Just add whatever you have lurking in the refrigerator.

1 tablespoon sesame oil
1 fresh red chili, seeded and finely chopped
1-inch piece fresh ginger root, peeled and chopped
1 bunch scallions, trimmed and sliced diagonally
1 yellow bell pepper, seeded and thinly sliced
1 green bell pepper, seeded and thinly sliced
1/4 pound parboiled baby corn
1/4 pound parboiled thin green beans
1/4 pound parboiled baby asparagus
pinch of five-spice powder
2 tablespoons soy sauce
1 tablespoon dry sherry
salt and freshly ground black pepper
1 tablespoon chopped cilantro leaves

FOR THE CRÊPES:
1 cup all-purpose flour
pinch of salt
1 egg
1¼ cups milk
oil for frying
2 tablespoons sesame seeds

1 Make the crêpe batter: sift the flour and salt into a bowl and mix in the egg and a little of the milk. Gradually beat in the remaining milk until you have a smooth batter. Let stand for 30 minutes before making the crêpes.

2 Heat a few drops of oil in a small skillet, and, when it is really hot, pour in a little of the batter, tilting the skillet to cover the base. Sprinkle with a few of the sesame seeds, and when the underside of the crêpe is set and golden, turn it over and cook the other side. Slide out of the skillet and keep warm. Cook the remaining crêpes in the same way.

3 Cover the crêpes in foil and keep them warm while you stir-fry the vegetables for the filling.

4 Heat the sesame oil in a wok or heavy skillet. Add the chili and ginger and stir-fry over medium heat for 1–2 minutes. Add the scallions and bell peppers, and stir-fry for 2–3 minutes. Stir in the parboiled vegetables and stir-fry for 1 minute.

5 Stir in the five-spice powder and then pour in the soy sauce and

Other crêpe fillings

1 Diced creamy blue cheese, e.g., gorgonzola, with wilted arugula and chopped toasted walnuts.

2 Sliced onions, fried slowly in butter until caramelized, and chopped parsley.

3 Button mushrooms in a herb-flecked creamy sauce.

4 Strips of red and yellow bell peppers sautéed in olive oil, with black olives, feta cheese, and herbs.

sherry. Stir-fry over high heat for 2 minutes, until the liquid evaporates. Season to taste with salt and pepper.

6 Place some of the stir-fried vegetables on each crêpe and fold over or roll up. Serve immediately sprinkled with chopped cilantro.

Serves 4

Spring rolls

Serves 4

A quick and easy way to make vegetable spring rolls is to use filo pastry rather than the usual wonton wrappers. The quantities are sufficient to make eight spring rolls for a main course, or twenty-four small bite-sized ones for passing round at happy hour with cocktails. If wished, you can prepare the spring rolls in advance and leave them in the refrigerator for a few hours before oiling and cooking them.

12 ounces filo pastry
vegetable oil for brushing
scallion tassels, to garnish
plum sauce or chili sauce,
for dipping

FOR THE FILLING:
2 tablespoons sesame oil
6 scallions, sliced diagonally
2 garlic cloves, crushed
1 fresh red chili, seeded and finely chopped

1-inch piece fresh ginger root, peeled and chopped
2 carrots, grated
1 cup shredded Chinese leaves or cabbage
1 cup bean sprouts
1 cup chopped mushrooms
2 tablespoons soy sauce
1 tablespoon dry sherry
pinch of sugar
1 tablespoon chopped parsley or cilantro leaves

1 Make the filling for the spring rolls. Heat the sesame oil in a wok and stir-fry the scallions, garlic, chili, and ginger for 2 minutes. Add the carrots, Chinese leaves or cabbage, bean sprouts, and mushrooms, and stir-fry for 2 minutes.

2 Add the soy sauce, sherry, and sugar and toss the vegetables in this mixture. Turn up the heat so that the liquid almost evaporates. Remove from the heat and leave to cool. Stir in the parsley or cilantro.

3 Unwrap the filo pastry, spread out one sheet and brush with oil — cover the remaining sheets with a damp cloth to prevent them drying

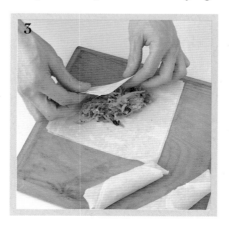

out. Cut the filo sheet in half and arrange some of the cooled vegetable filling along one side in a "sausage" shape. Turn the sides in over the edges of the filling and roll up to make a neat parcel. Assemble the other spring rolls in the same way.

4 Place the spring rolls on an oiled cookie sheet, brush with oil and cook in a preheated oven at 425°F for 12–15 minutes, until they are crisp and golden brown. Turn them over halfway through the cooking time. Serve the spring rolls immediately with scallion tassels and a plum or chili dipping sauce.

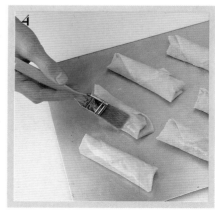

Fritto **Misto**

2 pounds prepared raw
vegetables, e.g., small fresh
artichokes, sliced eggplant,
zucchini batons, radicchio
quarters, mushrooms, or
parboiled vegetables, e.g.,
asparagus stalks, cauliflower
and broccoli florets, sliced
fennel, and celery
oil for deep-frying
ground sea salt
lemon wedges, to serve

FOR THE BATTER:
1 cup all-purpose flour
pinch of salt
1 tablespoon olive oil
1 cup water

An Italian *fritto misto* of mixed fried vegetables in a really crisp, light batter makes a memorable meal. You can use so many Mediterranean and seasonal vegetables, but the greatest delicacy of all, if you can get them, are orange zucchini blossoms. Serve the vegetable fritters with lemon wedges and a fresh tomato sauce, or a simple bowl of fromage frais into which you have stirred some red or green pesto sauce.

1 Make the batter: sift the flour and salt into a mixing bowl and make a hollow in the center. Mix in the olive oil and beat in the water. Beat well with a wooden spoon to make a smooth batter. Let stand for about 1 hour before using.

2 Prepare all the vegetables. Wash the raw ones, pat dry and leave whole, or cut or slice into smaller portions. Blanch the other vegetables in boiling water, then drain well and dry on paper towels.

3 Dip the vegetables quickly into the prepared batter and shake off any excess batter. Deep-fry in oil heated to 375°F for a few minutes, until crisp and golden. Remove with a slotted spoon, drain on paper towels and serve immediately, sprinkled with salt, with lemon wedges. A crisp salad of radicchio and bitter leaves tossed in a lemony olive oil dressing is the perfect accompaniment.

Serves 4

Layered **Nut** Roast

1 onion, finely chopped
2 garlic cloves, minced
4 tablespoons butter
1 cup ground Brazil nuts
1/3 cup ground hazelnuts
1 cup coarsely chopped shelled
sweet chestnuts
1 cup fresh whole-wheat
breadcrumbs
2 cups mashed
cooked parsnips or turnips
2 tablespoons chopped
fresh parsley
1 teaspoon chopped
fresh oregano
1 teaspoon fresh thyme leaves
1/2 teaspoon cayenne pepper

1 tablespoon mixed-nut butter
(almonds, hazelnuts, cashews)
grated rind and juice of 1 lemon
1 egg, beaten
3–4 tablespoons vegetable broth
salt and freshly ground
black pepper

FOR THE LAYERS:
1 cup thinly sliced white mushrooms
4 tablespoons butter
1/2 pound spinach
2/3 cup ricotta cheese
pinch of grated nutmeg
salt and freshly ground
black pepper

This lovely recipe is suitable for many celebrations and festive occasions. It is delicious served with a creamy mushroom sauce (see page 138), or you could eat it with cranberry sauce at either Christmas or Thanksgiving.

1 Fry the onion and garlic in the butter over low heat, until soft and golden. Transfer with a slotted spoon to a large mixing bowl.

2 Stir in the ground and chopped nuts, bread crumbs, mashed root vegetables, herbs, cayenne, nut butter, lemon rind, and juice. Bind

together with the beaten egg and vegetable broth, and season well.

3 Fry the mushrooms in the butter in a skillet until they are golden brown. Set aside to cool a little.

4 Pick over the spinach leaves, removing any thick stalks, and wash well to remove any dirt. Put in a saucepan, cover with a lid, and place over low heat. Cook for a few minutes until the spinach softens and turns bright green. Drain well, pressing out any moisture. Chop the drained spinach and mix with the ricotta cheese, nutmeg, and seasonings.

5 Butter a 2-pound loaf pan generously and spoon in one-third of the nut mixture. Press down well and cover with the fried mushrooms. Cover with half of the remaining mixture, and spread with the spinach

Fritto Misto

and ricotta. Top with the remaining nut mixture and level the top.

6 Bake in a preheated oven at 375°F for 45–50 minutes, until the nut roast is cooked and golden brown on top. Serve sliced with a creamy mushroom sauce (see page 138).

Serves 6–8

Garbanzo **Burritos**

These tortilla parcels are stuffed with a spicy filling of garbanzos, but you could use frijoles (refried beans, see page 50) instead. Like other Mexican dishes, they taste particularly good if served with a tomato salsa, guacamole (see page 141), and sour cream.

8 fresh flour tortillas
salsa (see page 16) or tomato
sauce (see page 32)
3/4 cup grated Cheddar cheese
guacamole and sour cream, to serve

FOR THE GARBANZO FILLING:
1 tablespoon vegetable oil
2 onions, chopped
1 garlic clove, minced

1 red bell pepper, seeded and chopped
1 small dried hot red chili, crumbled
3/4 cup skinned and chopped
tomatoes
1 tablespoon tomato paste
1 1/2 cups canned garbanzos, drained
salt and freshly ground black pepper
4 scallions, finely chopped
1 1/2 cups grated Cheddar cheese

1 Make the garbanzo filling. Heat the oil and fry the onions until soft and golden. Add the garlic and bell pepper and fry for 3–4 minutes, until softened. Stir in the chili, tomatoes, tomato paste, and drained garbanzos. Simmer for 8–10 minutes. Season to taste with salt and pepper.

2 Spread out the tortillas and place some of the garbanzo filling on each one. Sprinkle with the scallions and Cheddar cheese. Fold up each tortilla around the garbanzo filling like a

parcel, folding in the sides to seal it. Secure the burritos with wooden toothpicks and place them in a large buttered ovenproof dish.

3 Cover the dish with a sheet of kitchen foil and bake in a preheated oven at 350°F for 15 minutes. Remove the kitchen foil, spoon a little salsa or fresh tomato sauce over the top, sprinkle with grated Cheddar cheese and cook under a hot broiler, until the cheese is golden

brown and bubbling. Serve with guacamole and sour cream.

Serves 4

Other fillings

1 Grated Monterey Jack cheese, chopped hot green chilies and refried beans.

2 Grilled bell peppers and eggplant, cream cheese, and fresh cilantro.

Cheese and Potato Fritters

1 tablespoon olive oil
2 leeks, washed, trimmed,
and chopped
1 onion, finely chopped
1 cup chopped mushrooms
3 cups mashed potatoes, cooled
1 cup grated Monterey Jack or
Swiss cheese
3 tablespoons chopped fresh herbs,
e.g., parsley, chives, oregano, basil
salt and freshly ground
black pepper
3 tablespoons flour
pinch of cayenne pepper

olive oil for frying

FOR THE RED ONION
MARMALADE:
1 tablespoon butter
1 tablespoon olive oil
4 cups very thinly sliced
red onions
1 cup red wine
3 tablespoons wine vinegar
1 teaspoon sugar
salt and freshly ground
black pepper

This is a great way of using up cold mashed potatoes and small pieces of cheese. If you are calorie-conscious and don't want to fry the fritters, you can bake them for 15–20 minutes in a preheated oven at 375°F. Serve them with some piquant red onion marmalade and an arugula and radicchio (red chicory) salad.

1 Make the red onion marmalade: heat the butter and oil and cook the red onions over very low heat for

about 10 minutes until softened and almost caramelized. Add the wine, wine vinegar, and sugar and simmer gently for 30–40 minutes, until thick and reduced. Season to taste.

2 Heat the olive oil in a skillet and gently fry the leeks and onion until they are soft and golden. Stir in the mushrooms and fry for another 2–3 minutes. Drain off any surplus oil.

3 In a mixing bowl, mix the fried vegetables with the mashed potatoes, grated cheese, and herbs. Season to taste with salt and pepper, and then shape into 8 rounds.

4 Mix the flour and cayenne pepper, and use to dust the potato cakes. Heat some olive oil in a large skillet and fry the potato cakes over moderate heat until crisp and golden

Garbanzo Burritos

brown on both sides, turning them halfway through cooking.

5 Remove from the skillet and drain the hot fritters on paper towels. Serve them immediately with the red onion marmalade and a crisp salad.

Serves 4

Snacks & Fast Food

Vegetable stir-fries, quiches, tarts, pizzas, and toasts make healthy snacks and fast food.

Have fun experimenting with all the different toppings, fillings, and variations to create

new dishes that will become firm family favorites.

Thai Stir-fried **Vegetables**

3 tablespoons peanut oil
1 onion, sliced
3 garlic cloves, finely chopped
1 large fresh red or green chili,
seeded and sliced
2-inch piece fresh ginger root, peeled
and chopped
1 red bell pepper, seeded and sliced
1 green bell pepper, seeded and sliced
small bunch scallions,
trimmed and sliced
2–3 kaffir lime leaves, torn

4 ounces snow peas, trimmed
4 ounces baby corn
1/4 pound mushrooms, quartered,
e.g., white or shiitake
1 1/2 cups shredded green cabbage
2 tablespoons soy sauce
2 tablespoons rice wine or
dry sherry
1 teaspoon sugar
1 ounce fresh basil or cilantro leaves,
chopped
3/4 cup roasted cashews

You can make this dish as hot as you like by adding more chilies. Of course, you don't have to follow the recipe slavishly—the whole point of stir-fries is that you can add virtually any vegetables, herbs, or spices and still create a marvelous meal in minutes. In fact, the most time-consuming part of this dish is cutting and preparing all the vegetables.

1 Heat the peanut oil in a large wok or deep skillet. Add the onion, garlic, chili, and ginger, and then stir-fry over high heat for about 1 minute.

2 Add the bell peppers, scallions, and kaffir lime leaves, and stir-fry for 2–3 minutes. Then stir in the snow peas, baby corn, mushrooms, and cabbage. Continue stir-frying for 2 minutes. The vegetables should be heated through and just tender but should also still be slightly crisp.

3 Add the soy sauce, rice wine or sherry, and the sugar. Stir for 1–2 minutes to coat all the vegetables, then throw in the basil or cilantro and the roasted cashews. Serve immediately while the vegetables are still sizzling with fried noodles or some plain boiled rice.

Serves 4

Opposite: Stir-fried Vegetables

Greek **Spinach** Pie

You can eat this pie, layered with spinach, feta cheese, and filo pastry, either hot or cold. Good fruity olive oil, sweet butter, and salty feta cheese are essential for authenticity.

3 tablespoons extra-virgin olive oil
1 onion, thinly sliced
1 bunch scallions, trimmed
and thinly sliced
2 pounds fresh spinach, washed,
stalks removed, and shredded
4 tablespoons chopped flat-leaf
parsley

2 tablespoons chopped dill weed
4 medium eggs
8 ounces feta cheese, crumbled
3 tablespoons heavy cream
salt and freshly ground black pepper
pinch of grated nutmeg
4 tablespoons sweet butter, melted
1 pound filo pastry

1 Heat the olive oil and then fry the onion until soft and golden. Add the scallions and fry for 2–3 minutes. Stir in the shredded spinach until it is glistening with olive oil. Cover the pan and cook over gentle heat for 5 minutes. Stir in the parsley and dill weed, then remove the vegetables with a slotted spoon and drain well on paper towels.

2 Beat the eggs in a clean bowl and then stir in the feta cheese, cream, salt, pepper, and nutmeg. Mix with the drained, cooked vegetables.

3 Brush a 10-inch square baking pan with plenty of melted butter. Unfold the filo pastry and use a sheet to line the pan, trimming it to fit. Brush with melted butter, then lay another sheet on top. Build up another 4 or 5 layers in this way, buttering between each one.

4 Cover with the cheese and spinach mixture and level the top. Cover with another 4 or 5 sheets of filo pastry, buttering between the sheets.

Brush the top layer generously with the remaining melted butter, and mark it into serving portions with the point of a sharp knife, cutting just through the top 2 layers of filo.

5 Bake in a preheated oven at 350°F for about 40 minutes, until the filo pastry is puffed up, crisp, and golden brown. Serve hot or cold with a crisp green salad.

Serves 6

Vegetable Tatin

This is a savory variation on the classic sweet tarte tatin, which is made with apples or pears.

1 green bell pepper
1 yellow bell pepper
2 tablespoons butter
1 tablespoon sugar
1 tablespoon white wine vinegar
2 pounds red onions, peeled
1 tablespoon chopped rosemary
and thyme
salt and freshly ground
black pepper
8 ounces puff pastry

1 Grill the bell peppers until the skin is blistered and charred. Skin them, removing the stalks and seeds. Cut into large chunks.

2 Melt the butter in a large, shallow, flameproof pan over moderate heat. Stir in the sugar and wine vinegar. Cut the onions in half and arrange them, on their sides, in the buttery mixture in the base of the pan, packing them in quite tightly.

3 Tuck the bell peppers between the onions and sprinkle with the chopped herbs, salt, and pepper. Cook gently for 5 minutes. Cover the pan and cook in a preheated oven at 350°F

for 30–40 minutes. Remove the vegetable tatin from the oven and increase the temperature to 400°F.

4 Roll out the pastry and cut out a round or oval, depending on the shape of the pan—it should be a little larger than the pan. Place the pastry on top of the onions and tuck in the edges round the inside of the pan.

5 Return to the hot oven and bake for 25–30 minutes, until the puff pastry is well risen, crisp, and golden. Cool before inverting the dish and turning out the tatin.

Serves 4-6

Mushroom and Goat's Cheese Tart

Tarts and quiches make versatile vegetarian food because there are so many different fillings you can use. If you don't like goat's cheese, you can use Swiss or Monterey Jack instead.

2¼ cups all-purpose flour
pinch of salt
1 stick butter, diced
1 egg yolk
cold water, to mix

FOR THE FILLING
2 tablespoons butter
1 onion, chopped
2½ cups thinly sliced mushrooms
4 ounces firm goat's cheese
2 large eggs
1 egg yolk
1¼ cups heavy cream
pinch of grated nutmeg
2 tablespoons chopped parsley
and chives
salt and freshly ground
black pepper

1 Make the pie crust: sift the flour and salt into a mixing bowl and rub in the butter until the mixture resembles fine bread crumbs. Stir in the egg yolk and enough cold water to mix to a smooth, well blended ball of dough, which leaves the sides of the bowl clean.

Variations

You can fill the pie shell with one of the following alternative fillings and then pour the egg and cream mixture over the top and bake in the same way.

1 Onions (2 pounds) cooked slowly over low heat until caramelized.

2 Cooked fresh spinach and cream cheese.

3 Young asparagus boiled until tender with grated Swiss cheese.

4 Sautéed sliced leeks and bell peppers with sun-dried tomatoes and herbs.

5 Sautéed sliced zucchini, rosemary, and grated Cheddar cheese.

6 Crumbled blue cheese, chopped chives, and thinly sliced scallions.

7 Thinly sliced tomatoes, chopped fresh herbs, and grated Swiss, mozzarella, or Cheddar cheese.

8 Fresh peas, baby asparagus, canned artichoke hearts, cream cheese, chopped tarragon and chervil.

9 Broccoli florets, grated nutmeg, and Swiss cheese.

10 Sautéed sliced onions, garlic, roasted red bell pepper strips, pitted black olives, and grated cheese.

2 Wrap the dough in some plastic wrap or waxed paper and let rest in the refrigerator for 15 minutes.

3 Roll out the dough on a lightly floured surface and use to line a buttered 10-inch fluted springform pie pan. Chill in the refrigerator for at least 15 minutes, then line with waxed paper or crumpled kitchen foil and fill with baking beans. Bake in a preheated oven at 350°F for 15–20 minutes. Remove the paper or foil and beans. Leave to cool.

4 Make the mushroom and goat's cheese filling: heat the butter in a skillet and then fry the onion gently over low heat until softened and golden. Add the mushrooms and continue cooking for 10–15 minutes, until they are softened and turning golden brown. Drain off any of the pan juices.

5 Spoon the onion and mushrooms evenly over the base of the baked pie

crust and then scatter with the crumbled goat's cheese.

6 Beat the eggs, egg yolk, and cream together. Season with nutmeg and stir in the parsley and chives. Add a little salt and pepper, and pour over the mushroom filling.

7 Place the tart on a cookie sheet and bake in a preheated oven at 350°F for 30–40 minutes, until the filling is just set and still ever so slightly wobbly. Serve the tart warm or cold, cut into wedges, with a crisp green salad.

Serves 6

Loaded **Potato** Skins

You can top scooped-out baked potatoes with a variety of different toppings. Serve as a snack or as a main meal with salad. Don't throw away the potato flesh. Mash it up with some olive oil and minced garlic or use to make Cheese and Potato Fritters (see page 76).

8 medium-sized baking potatoes
2 tablespoons butter
salt and freshly ground
black pepper
2 cups grated Monterey Jack or
Swiss cheese

TO SERVE:
shredded lettuce, salsa (see page 16), and guacamole (see page 141)

1 Scrub the potatoes and bake in a preheated oven at 400°F for about 1 hour, until tender.

2 Cut each potato in half lengthwise and scoop out most of the flesh, leaving a little potato around the inside of each shell. Spread a little butter inside the potatoes and season with salt and pepper.

3 Fill the hollow in each potato half with grated cheese and place the potatoes, cheese-side up, in a foil-lined broiler pan. Cook under a preheated hot broiler for 5 minutes, until the filling is golden brown and bubbling.

4 Serve the potato skins with some shredded lettuce, hot salsa, and guacamole.

Serves 4

Variations

You can fill the scooped-out potatoes with any of the following:

1 Chopped tomatoes and scallions, then sprinkle with cheese and broil.

2 Sour cream, chopped scallions, and chopped chives.

3 Fromage frais mixed with chopped fresh cilantro and diced avocado.

4 Frijoles (see page 50), then top with grated cheese and broil.

5 Soft goat's cheese mixed with grilled bell peppers and chopped herbs.

6 Homemade coleslaw.

7 Creamy fromage frais blended with green or red pesto sauce.

Nachos with Guacamole

These Tex-Mex snacks are now popular all over the United States. Serve them at happy hour with cocktails or as party food.

1 Heat the oil and gently fry the onion and garlic until soft and golden. Add the tomatoes, chilies, cumin, and sugar, and simmer until the sauce reduces and thickens. Season to taste with salt and pepper.

2 Arrange the tortilla chips on a large, shallow ovenproof dish, and spoon the chili sauce over the top, putting a little on each one. Sprinkle the grated cheese over them and bake the nachos in a preheated oven at 350°F for 5–10

2 tablespoons vegetable oil
1 onion, chopped
2 garlic cloves, minced
4 large tomatoes, skinned and chopped
2 fresh green chilies, seeded and chopped
pinch of ground cumin
pinch of sugar
salt and freshly ground black pepper

8 ounces tortilla chips
1 cup grated Cheddar or Monterey Jack cheese
5/8 cup sour cream
3/4 cup guacamole (see page 141)
diced onion and tomato, to garnish
1 fresh green chili, seeded and cut into slivers

minutes, until the cheese melts and starts to bubble.

3 Serve the nachos piping hot with bowls of sour cream and guacamole, garnished with diced onion and

tomato, and slivers of hot green chili so guests can help themselves.

Serves 4-6

Opposite: Nachos with Guacamole

Mediterranean Vegetable Tart

Serves 6

This colorful tart is full of the bold flavors of the Mediterranean: luscious tomatoes, vibrant bell peppers, fresh young zucchini, and velvety eggplants. Serve the tart with a lightly dressed green salad and some crusty bread for a perfect lunch.

8 ounces pie crust dough (page 141)
½ cup grated vegetarian Parmesan
or Cheddar cheese
1 tablespoon olive oil
few sprigs of basil and oregano

FOR THE FILLING:
1 medium eggplant, cubed
2 zucchini, cubed
3 tablespoons olive oil
1 small onion, finely chopped

1 small red bell pepper, seeded and
diced
1 small yellow bell pepper, seeded
and diced
2 garlic cloves, minced
1½ cups skinned and chopped ripe
tomatoes
1 tablespoon tomato paste
pinch of sugar
salt and freshly ground
black pepper.

1 Roll out the pie crust dough on a lightly floured surface and use to line a greased 10-inch deep pie pan. Prick the base with a fork and line with kitchen foil and baking beans. Bake in a preheated oven at 400°F for 15 minutes. Remove the foil and beans and set aside to cool.

2 Meanwhile, make the filling. Put the eggplant and zucchini in a colander and sprinkle with salt. Leave for 20 minutes to exude their bitter juices. Rinse them well under cold running water and then pat dry with paper towels.

3 Heat the oil and sauté the onion gently until soft and transparent, without coloring. Add the bell peppers and garlic and cook gently for 2–3 minutes, stirring occasionally. Add the eggplant and zucchini, and cook gently for 5 minutes. Stir in the tomatoes, tomato paste, and sugar. Cook over low heat for 5–10

minutes, until the tomato sauce has reduced and thickened slightly. Season to taste with salt and pepper.

4 Fill the pie crust with the cooked vegetable mixture. Sprinkle the grated Parmesan or Cheddar cheese over the top, and then drizzle with the olive oil. Bake the tart in a preheated oven at 400°F for about 20–25 minutes. If the tart looks as though it is browning too much, cover it with some kitchen foil and then reduce the oven temperature to 350°F. Serve the tart warm, garnished with little sprigs of basil and oregano.

Pizza

If you're in a hurry, you can use a ready-made pizza base, but it doesn't taste as good as the real thing. Making the dough does not take very long, but you have to allow time for it to rise. Alternatively, you can rustle up a quick pizza with a vacuum-packed pizza base, a pita bread, a toasted English muffin, or some sliced ciabatta brushed with olive oil and then toasted. Cover with one of the suggested toppings and then bake in a preheated oven or cook under a hot broiler, and you can eat really delicious, healthy fast food.

1 envelope dry yeast
1¼ cups warm water
4½ cups bread flour
1 teaspoon salt
2 tablespoons olive oil

FOR THE TOPPING:
4 tablespoons olive oil
1 garlic clove, minced
1½ cups canned chopped tomatoes
1 tablespoon tomato paste
1 tablespoon chopped oregano
salt and freshly ground
black pepper
6 pieces sun-dried tomatoes
in oil, sliced
1 cup sliced onion or mushrooms
(optional)
½ cup pitted black olives
8 ounces mozzarella cheese, thinly
sliced

1 Sprinkle the yeast over the warm water; let stand for 10 minutes, until foamy. Sift the flour and salt into a large bowl, make a well in the center and pour in the blended yeast and oil. Gradually add the flour and mix to a soft dough.

2 Turn out the dough onto a lightly floured surface and knead well until it is smooth, pliable, and elastic. Place the ball of dough in a bowl, cover with a cloth, and leave in a warm place for 1 hour, until well risen and doubled in size.

3 Turn out the dough onto a lightly floured surface, punch it down, and divide into 4 pieces. Knead each piece lightly and roll out until it is about 12 inches in diameter. Place each pizza on an oiled metal cookie sheet and brush with a little olive oil.

4 While the dough is rising, make the tomato sauce for the topping. Heat 2 tablespoons of the olive oil and toss the garlic in it. Add the tomatoes and simmer for 15 minutes, or until the sauce is thick and reduced. Stir in the tomato paste, oregano, and seasoning.

Pizza toppings
....

Here are some ideas for delicious toppings.
....

1 Over the tomato sauce, scatter thinly sliced onion rings, capers, golden raisins, pine nuts, and olives. Top with sliced mozzarella cheese.
....

2 Brush the base with olive oil and scatter with sliced cherry tomatoes, basil, olives, and crumbled goat's cheese.
....

3 Over the tomato sauce, arrange oiled chunks of eggplant and zucchini and thinly sliced red onions. Sprinkle with chopped oregano and mozzarella.
....

4 Brush the base with green or red pesto sauce and top with char-grilled bell peppers and grated pizza cheese.
....

5 Arrange some sautéed leeks over the tomato sauce and sprinkle with diced fontina and crumbled ricotta cheeses.
....

5 Spread the tomato sauce over the pizzas and scatter the sun-dried tomatoes, sliced onion or mushrooms (if using), and olives over the top. Finally, scatter the mozzarella cheese over the topping and drizzle with the remaining olive oil.

6 Bake in a preheated oven at 425°F for 12–15 minutes, until the base of the pizza is cooked through, crisp and golden brown.

Serves 4

Opposite: Pizza

Bruschetta with Garlic

The ultimate quick snack—grilled garlic-flavored, crusty country bread with a delicious savory topping.

8 slices crusty country-style bread
2 garlic cloves, peeled and halved
4 tablespoons fruity olive oil
sea salt

1 Grill or toast the slices of bread on both sides, then rub one side of each slice with the cut garlic cloves.

2 Drizzle the olive oil over the top, sprinkle with sea salt and enjoy, or top with one of the suggested savory toppings (right).

Serves 4

Toppings for bruschetta

1 Grilled sliced red and yellow bell peppers with ground black pepper.

2 Chopped ripe tomatoes and basil or oregano.

3 Sliced tomato, black olives, and grilled goat's cheese.

4 Scrambled eggs and chives.

5 Caramelized onions to which balsamic vinegar has been added.

6 Red onion marmalade (see page 76).

7 Pesto sauce and mozzarella.

8 Olive tapenade or sun-dried tomato paste, radicchio, and grilled Taleggio.

9 Creamed mushrooms (see page 24).

10 Walnuts, watercress, and creamy Gorgonzola or blue cheese.

11 Eggplant slices brushed with olive oil, then grilled.

12 Cottage cheese or ricotta with lots of chopped herbs.

Crostini Toasts

These are often confused with bruschetta, but they are much smaller. Use a thinly sliced French breadstick to make these wonderful "little toasts." They are ideal for parties, or for serving with cocktails before dinner. Like bruschetta, you can top them with a wide range of different toppings.

1 small French breadstick (flute)
4–5 tablespoons olive oil
sea salt

1 Slice the bread thinly and toast one side under a preheated hot broiler.

2 Brush the untoasted side of each slice of bread with olive oil and put back under the broiler until crisp and golden.

3 Sprinkle with a little sea salt and top with any one of the suggested bruschetta toppings (above) or one of the savory ideas (right).

Serves 4–6

Toppings for crostini

1 Hummus sprinkled with paprika, lemon juice, and olive oil.

2 Sliced pear, arugula, and creamy goat's cheese.

3 Tsatsiki, grilled eggplant, and chopped fresh mint.

4 Pan-fried sliced apple and blue cheese.

5 Fried tofu, chili sauce, fresh cilantro, and grilled cheese.

6 Sun-dried tomato paste with feta cheese.

Mozzarella in Carrozza

This is the perfect snack food for eating "on the hoof" as thousands of people in Rome and other Italian cities do on their way to work each morning. Use only the real Italian mozzarella packed in water.

8 slices of white bread
8 ounces mozzarella, drained and sliced
2 large eggs
2 tablespoons milk
olive oil for frying

1 Cut the crusts off the bread. Divide the mozzarella between 4 slices of the bread and cover with the remaining slices. Press them firmly together.

2 Beat the eggs and milk together in a bowl, and then dip the mozzarella

sandwiches briefly into this mixture. They should soak up the egg on both sides.

3 Fry the sandwiches, one at a time, in hot olive oil in a skillet for 3–4 minutes each side, until crisp and golden. Drain on paper towels, and cook the remaining sandwiches in the same way. Cut each sandwich in half and eat immediately.

Serves 4

Stuffed **Croissants**

Buttery, flaky croissants (crescent rolls) can be warmed through and filled with a savory mixture, or topped with grated cheese and cooked under a preheated hot broiler. Alternatively, you can fill them with fruit or chocolate for a sweet snack or quick dessert.

4 croissants
1 quantity creamy mushrooms
(see page 24)
¼ cup grated Swiss cheese

1 Place the croissants under a hot broiler or in a preheated oven at 350°F for a few minutes, just long enough to warm them through.

2 Then split the croissants in half lengthwise and fill with the hot creamy mushroom mixture. Sandwich them back together and sprinkle the tops with grated cheese.

Savory fillings

1 Put some sliced Cheddar or Swiss cheese on both sides of the croissants, put back under the broiler until the cheese melts and sandwich together with sliced tomato or watercress. Alternatively, use plum tomatoes and Mozzarella.

2 Fill with fried sliced onions, and mushrooms topped with Dijon mustard and melted cheese.

3 Fill the croissants with creamy scrambled eggs and sautéed sliced button mushrooms sprinkled with chopped parsley.

4 Spread the split croissants with mayonnaise or natural fromage frais and then fill with shredded crisp lettuce, feta cheese, and avocado.

Sweet fillings

1 Fill with mascarpone cheese and shavings of really dark chocolate, then flash under a hot broiler to melt the chocolate.

2 Fill with apple sauce or pears cooked in

butter and sweetened with brown sugar, and crème fraîche.

3 Fill with fromage frais or ricotta and fresh raspberries dusted with sugar.

3 Place the croissants under the hot broiler or replace them in the oven for 2–3 minutes, until the cheese melts.

Serves 4

Beanburgers and Red Pepper Relish

You can make delicious burgers with puréed beans, garbanzo peas, and lentils. Serve straight out of the pan with bell pepper relish.

1 Put the beans in a bowl, cover with cold water and leave them to soak overnight. Drain and place in a saucepan with fresh water. Bring to a boil, then simmer for 1–1 1/4 hours, until tender. Drain well and then set aside to cool.

2 Meanwhile, make the bell pepper relish. Gently fry the onion in the olive oil until golden. Add the sugar and balsamic vinegar, turn up the heat and cook quickly until the liquid evaporates and turns syrupy. Grill or roast the bell peppers and garlic cloves. Skin, seed, and chop the bell peppers. Peel and mash the garlic cloves. Stir the chopped bell peppers, mashed garlic flesh, and cilantro into the onion mixture. Season to taste.

3 Put the cooled beans in a food processor or blender with the onion, garlic, chili (if using), parsley, egg,

1 1/3 cups dried white beans or cannellini beans
1 small onion, chopped
2 garlic cloves, minced
1 fresh red chili, chopped (optional)
few sprigs of parsley
1 egg
pinch of grated nutmeg
3/4 cup grated Swiss cheese
2 tablespoons fromage frais
squeeze of lemon juice
salt and freshly ground black pepper
oil for frying

FOR THE COATING:
1 egg, beaten
2 cups fresh bread crumbs

FOR THE BELL PEPPER RELISH:
1 onion, chopped
2 tablespoons olive oil
pinch of sugar
1 tablespoon balsamic vinegar
2 red bell peppers
2 garlic cloves
1 tablespoon chopped fresh cilantro
salt and freshly ground black pepper

nutmeg, and grated Swiss cheese. Process until puréed, then add the fromage frais, a squeeze of lemon juice, and some salt and pepper.

4 Chill the bean mixture in the refrigerator for at least 30 minutes, then divide it into 8 or 12 portions and, with floured hands, shape each one into a round.

5 Dip each round in beaten egg and then into the bread crumbs, until

evenly coated. Fry in hot oil until crisp and golden on both sides. Drain on paper towels. Serve hot with the warm bell pepper relish.

Serves 6

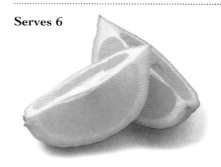

Spiced Onion Rings

Serve these red-hot fried onion rings with vegetable burgers or beanburgers (above).

1 Put the onion rings in a bowl and pour the milk over the top. Leave to soak for at least 30 minutes. Remove the onions and drain well.

2 Mix the flour, cornstarch, chili powder, paprika, salt, and sugar in a

shallow dish. Dip the onions in the seasoned flour, shaking off any excess flour.

3 Quickly deep-fry the onions in hot oil at 375°F, until they are evenly crisp and golden. Remove with a slotted spoon and drain on paper towels. Serve the onion rings immediately.

Serves 4–6

4 large onions, thinly sliced in rings
5/8 cup milk
1 cup all-purpose flour
2 tablespoons cornstarch
2 teaspoons hot chili powder
1 teaspoon paprika
good pinch of salt
pinch of sugar
oil for deep frying

Cajun Grilled **Vegetables**

Grilled blackened vegetables sprinkled with cajun spices can be served simply with sour cream or yogurt flavored with mint.

4 plum tomatoes, halved
2 eggplants, sliced
2 red onions, quartered
1 pound pumpkin, peeled, seeded, and sliced
2 red bell peppers, seeded and quartered
2 tablespoons pine nuts
$^1/_2$ cup olive oil
1 tablespoon ground cajun spices
sea salt and black pepper

FOR THE SALAD GARNISH:
$^1/_4$ pound peppery salad leaves,

e.g., arugula, watercress
3 tablespoons extra-virgin olive oil
1 tablespoon balsamic vinegar
4 ounces feta cheese, cubed

FOR THE SAUCE:
$^5/_8$ cup thick plain yogurt or sour cream
squeeze of lemon juice
3 tablespoons finely chopped fresh mint
freshly ground sea salt and ground black pepper

1 Prepare all the vegetables and spread them out in a broiler pan lined with foil, or on a hot grill. Scatter with pine nuts and drizzle with olive oil, paying particular attention to the eggplants. Sprinkle the cajun spices evenly over the top.

2 Cook under a hot broiler or on a grill until the vegetables are tender and charred, but not burnt. Turn the eggplants, tomatoes, and pumpkin over when they look golden brown and slightly charred around the edges on one side. Brush occasionally with the spicy olive oil in the broiler pan. Season with salt and pepper.

3 Wash and spin the salad leaves. Mix the olive oil and balsamic vinegar, and toss the leaves and feta cheese in this dressing. Arrange on a serving plate with the hot cajun grilled vegetables.

4 Mix the yogurt or sour cream with the lemon juice, mint, and seasoning to taste. Serve chilled with the grilled vegetables and salad.

Serves 4

Roasted Italian-style **Mushrooms**

Large white mushrooms make a delicious snack on toast. If possible, use Italian Fontina cheese in this recipe, as it melts to a wonderful consistency.

8 large 4-inch diameter white mushrooms
3 tablespoons olive oil
2 tablespoons chopped parsley
1 tablespoon chopped chives
2 garlic cloves, minced
salt and freshly ground black pepper
8 slices crusty round bread
12 ounces Fontina cheese

1 Arrange the mushrooms, stalk side up, in a kitchen foil-lined broiler pan. Mix the olive oil with the herbs and garlic, and brush gently over the mushrooms. Season with salt and freshly ground black pepper.

2 Place under a preheated hot broiler for about 4–5 minutes, until the mushrooms are heated through and softened. Remove and cut each mushroom into $^1/_2$-inch wide strips.

3 Toast the bread lightly on both sides. Slice the Fontina cheese into $^1/_2$-inch wide strips. Arrange the strips of mushroom and

Fontina alternately on the slices of toasted bread.

4 Place the toasts on a cookie sheet and bake in a preheated hot oven at 400°F for 5 minutes. Serve the mushroom toasts immediately.

Serves 4

Side Dishes & Salads

The following recipes for vegetable side dishes and some sensational salads can be served as an accompaniment to the main meal. They are incredibly varied, including baked gratins, fritters, stir fries, and even a barbecued salad.

Provençal **Vegetable** Gratin

You can make a gratin with almost any vegetable. They can be layered, or mixed into a creamy sauce, or moistened with vegetable broth or cream, but they must be baked in an oiled or buttered ovenproof dish until tender, and topped with crisp bread crumbs and grated cheese.

1 Place the eggplant slices in a colander and sprinkle with salt. Set aside for 30 minutes to drain their bitter juices. Rinse well under cold running water and then pat dry with some paper towels.

2 Fry the sliced eggplant, onions and garlic in 5 tablespoons of the olive oil until golden brown. Spread the fried vegetables over the base of a shallow ovenproof dish.

3 With a potato peeler, carefully remove strips of peel lengthwise from the sides of the zucchini to

1 eggplant, sliced
2 onions, thinly sliced
2 garlic cloves, minced
6 tablespoons olive oil
3 large zucchini
3 large tomatoes, skinned and sliced
salt and freshly ground black pepper
1 tablespoon chopped thyme and rosemary

FOR THE TOPPING:
4 tablespoons fresh white bread crumbs
2 tablespoons grated vegetarian Parmesan cheese
1 tablespoon olive oil

leave vertical green stripes and then slice the zucchini thinly.

4 Arrange the zucchini and tomatoes in alternate rows on top of the eggplant mixture, overlapping them like fish scales. Brush lightly with the remaining olive oil, season, and

Other vegetable gratins

1 Thinly sliced potatoes layered with chopped onion and garlic, moistened with vegetable broth or boiling milk and cream, and sprinkled with bread crumbs and grated Swiss cheese.

2 Sliced chayote cooked until tender, drenched in a creamy white sauce and scattered with chopped parsley, bread crumbs, paprika, and grated cheese, then browned under a hot broiler.

then scatter with the chopped herbs.

5 Bake in a preheated oven at 375°F for 20 minutes. Remove from the oven and sprinkle with bread crumbs and Parmesan cheese, drizzle with olive oil, and then bake for a further 10 minutes, until crisp and golden.

Serves 4

Opposite: Provençal Vegetable Gratin

Baked **Fennel** Niçoise

4 large round fennel bulbs
2 tablespoons butter
1 tablespoon olive oil
1/2 cup fresh bread crumbs
1 tablespoon grated vegetarian
Parmesan cheese
salt and freshly ground
black pepper
1 tablespoon chopped fennel leaves
or flat-leaf parsley

This dish has a delicious aniseed flavor but works well with celery.

1 Cut off the bases and hard stalks of the fennel bulbs, reserving any feathery leaves. Wash thoroughly and then cut each bulb in half from top to bottom.

2 Cook the fennel in boiling salted water for 15–20 minutes, until just tender but not soft. Drain well and leave to cool.

3 Cut the cooled fennel lengthwise into thick slices and arrange them, overlapping each other, in a buttered ovenproof dish. Dot them with butter and drizzle the olive oil over the top. Sprinkle with the bread crumbs and grated Parmesan cheese, then season.

4 Bake in a preheated oven at 400°F for 15 minutes, until golden brown. Sprinkle the chopped fennel or flat-leaf parsley over the top.

Serves 4–6

French **Potato** Bake

This is really easy to assemble and can be made well in advance for cooking later. For a really special variation, add some soaked dried porcini to the potatoes and sprinkle the top with grated cheese.

2 pounds potatoes
1 onion, finely chopped
1 leek, washed, trimmed, and
finely chopped
2 garlic cloves, minced
salt and freshly ground
black pepper
1 1/4 cups hot vegetable broth (or
stock and milk)
3 tablespoons butter, diced
1 tablespoon finely
chopped parsley

1 Peel the potatoes and slice them thinly lengthwise. Cover the base of a buttered ovenproof dish with a layer of potato slices.

2 Sprinkle some of the chopped onion and leek over the potatoes, then scatter a little garlic and seasoning over the top. Continue layering in this way until all the vegetables are used up, finishing with a layer of potatoes.

3 Pour the hot vegetable broth

slowly over the potatoes, so that it all sinks in. If wished, you can now cover the potato bake with some kitchen foil and set aside in a cool place until needed.

4 When ready to cook, dot the top of the potato bake with some butter, and bake in a preheated oven at 350°F for 30–40 minutes, until the top is crisp and golden brown. Sprinkle the potato bake with chopped parsley before serving.

Serves 4

Other vegetable bakes

1 Drained, cooked cauliflower or broccoli coated in a blue cheese sauce, sprinkled with bread crumbs and grated Parmesan cheese and broiled until browned.

2 Sliced boiled beetroot layered with grated cheese, covered in cream and topped with

bread crumbs and cheese. Dot with butter and bake for 10–15 minutes.

3 Sliced or puréed cooked pumpkin, layered with grated Swiss cheese, sprinkled with bread crumbs and grated cheese, then dotted with butter and baked for 5–10 minutes.

Rosemary-scented **Zucchini**

This is a lovely aromatic summer dish. Plain boiled, steamed, or fried zucchinis can be dull, but the addition of fresh rosemary and some cream transforms them into something special.

2 pounds zucchini
2 tablespoons fruity green
olive oil
1 tablespoon butter
few sprigs of fresh rosemary
5/8 cup crème fraîche
salt and freshly ground black pepper

1 Trim the ends off the zucchini and slice them thickly. Cook them in lightly salted boiling water for 3–4 minutes, and then drain well.

2 Heat the olive oil and butter in a saucepan, and add the drained zucchini and sprigs of rosemary. Cover the pan and cook very gently over low heat for about 5 minutes, until the zucchini are just starting to turn golden.

3 Stir in the crème fraîche carefully without damaging the zucchini, and cook gently for about 5 minutes, until the sauce reduces and the zucchini are tender. Season to taste with salt and lots of freshly ground black pepper. Serve immediately.

Serves 4-6

Louisiana **Sweetcorn** Fritters

These little crunchy fritters from the Deep South of the United States go well with most vegetable and bean chili dishes, or they can be served as a savory snack with cocktails or at parties.

1/2 cup all-purpose flour
pinch of salt
1 egg, beaten
4–5 tablespoons milk
1 cup drained canned
corn kernels
1 small green bell pepper, seeded
and finely chopped
1 small fresh red chili, seeded
and finely chopped
pinch of paprika
peanut oil or sweet
butter for frying

TO SERVE:
salsa, guacamole, sour cream,
chopped red onion, lime wedges

1 Sift the flour and salt into a bowl and beat in the egg. Add enough milk, beating well, to make a really smooth batter with a thick, creamy consistency. Let stand for at least 30 minutes before making the fritters.

2 Stir the corn kernels, green bell pepper, chili, and paprika into the batter, then drop a few spoonfuls of the mixture into some hot peanut oil or butter. Fry gently until golden brown underneath and then turn the fritters over and cook the other side.

3 Remove the hot cooked fritters, drain on paper towels, and keep warm. Cook the remaining fritters in the hot oil in the same way until all the batter is used up.

4 Serve the fritters very hot with salsa, guacamole, or chopped avocado, sour cream, chopped red onion, and wedges of lime.

Serves 6

Roasted Winter **Vegetables**

2 medium carrots, peeled
and halved
4 small parsnips
1 small swede or 4 turnips, peeled
and cut into wedges
2 potatoes, peeled and
cut into wedges
1 pound pumpkin, peeled, seeded,
and sliced thickly
2 fat leeks, washed, trimmed,
and quartered
2 sweet potatoes, peeled and sliced
4 stalks celery,
cut into large chunks
few sprigs of thyme or rosemary
sea salt and ground black pepper
1 garlic clove, minced
4–5 tablespoons olive oil

Most winter root vegetables lend themselves well to roasting. Serve them with quiches, grilled tofu, nut roast, or beanburgers, or on their own with fromage frais and chili sauce. You don't have to follow the recipe—just use the seasonal vegetables of your choice.

1 Prepare all the vegetables and spread them out in a large roasting pan or shallow ovenproof dish. Tuck the herbs down between the vegetables and sprinkle with sea salt and pepper and the minced garlic. Drizzle the olive oil over the top and turn the vegetables gently in the oil.

2 Roast in a preheated hot oven at 400°F for 30–40 minutes, until all the vegetables are cooked and tender.

Serves 4–6

Roasted summer vegetables

Roasted vegetables taste equally good in summer, especially served outside with salads and grilled food. Roast them in exactly the same way; choose from the following: asparagus, eggplants, corn, zucchini, mushrooms, onions, bell peppers, red onions, and tomatoes. Sprinkle with oregano, marjoram, rosemary, and olive oil before roasting.

Roman **Cauliflower**

1 large cauliflower
4 tablespoons extra-virgin
olive oil
2 fresh red chilies, seeded
and finely chopped
(or 2 dried chilies)
salt and freshly ground
black pepper

This hot, spicy way of cooking cauliflower is popular in Rome. You can cook romanesco cauliflowers, broccoli, Swiss chard, pak choi, and winter leafy green vegeetables in the same way.

1 Cut off the thick stalk and outer leaves from the cauliflower. Cut in half, remove the core, and divide the cauliflower into florets.

2 Cook the florets in lightly salted boiling water until just tender but still very firm. Drain well and then dry on paper towels.

3 Heat the olive oil in a large skillet. Add the chilies and fry very gently over

low heat for about 5 minutes to flavor the oil.

4 Add the drained cauliflower florets and stir gently in the hot oil until evenly covered. Turn up the heat a little and cook for a few minutes, until heated through. Sprinkle some freshly ground black pepper over the cauliflower florets and serve them immediately.

Serves 4

Opposite: Roasted Winter Vegetables

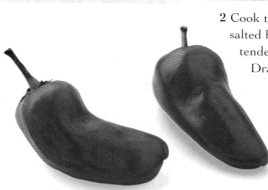

Hungarian Lecso

3 tablespoons olive oil
1 large onion, thinly sliced
4 green bell peppers, seeded and sliced
4 large ripe tomatoes, skinned and chopped
2 teaspoons sugar
1 tablespoon paprika
salt and black pepper
1 tablespoon chopped flat-leaf parsley

TO SERVE:
sour cream and caraway seeds

In Hungary, plain boiled or steamed vegetables are unknown. The Hungarians love rich, colorful vegetable stews, flavored with spices or fresh seasonal fruit. Lecso is characteristic of their fiery, distinctive style of cooking. Be sure to use really ripe red tomatoes and good-quality paprika in this dish.

1 Heat the olive oil and fry the onion gently over low heat until softened and golden. Stir in the bell peppers and simmer for 10–15 minutes, until the bell peppers are soft.

2 Stir in the tomatoes, sugar, and paprika, and continue cooking for about 15 minutes, until the mixture thickens and reduces. Season to taste with salt and pepper, and add another pinch of sugar if necessary.

3 Serve hot sprinkled with flat-leaf parsley, with a spoonful of sour cream and some caraway seeds.

Serves 4

Green Beans with Chilies

If you get bored with boiled green beans, try this delicious Chinese stir-fried dish. Serve it with rice or noodles.

1 Trim the beans and remove the "strings" along their sides. Heat the oil in a wok or deep skillet, and add the garlic, ginger, and chilies. Stir-fry for 1 minute over moderate heat. Stir in the scallions and salt, and continue stir-frying for 1 minute.

2 Add the green beans and cashews, and stir-fry for 1 minute. Add the

1 pound thin green beans
3 tablespoons corn or sesame oil
2 garlic cloves, minced
1-inch piece fresh ginger root, peeled and chopped
2 fresh red chilies, seeded and finely chopped
4 scallions, trimmed and sliced
good pinch of salt
1/4 cup cashews
1/2 cup vegetable broth
2 tablespoons light soy sauce
1 tablespoon sherry
1 teaspoon sugar
freshly ground black pepper

vegetable broth, soy sauce, sherry, and sugar, and turn up the heat. When the liquid starts to boil, reduce the heat and let it simmer for 4–5 minutes, stirring occasionally, until the liquid reduces and the beans are tender. Sprinkle with plenty of black pepper and serve.

Serves 4

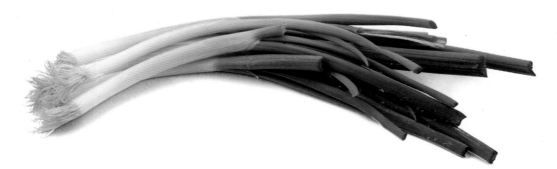

Indian Spiced **Potatoes**

1¹/2 pounds potatoes, peeled
4–5 tablespoons vegetable oil
1 fresh chili, finely chopped
2 garlic cloves, minced
¹/2 teaspoon cumin seeds
¹/2 teaspoon mustard seeds
1 teaspoon ground turmeric
¹/2 teaspoon salt
¹/4 teaspoon chili powder

TO SERVE:
¹/2 cup plain yogurt
1 tablespoon chopped
fresh cilantro
mango chutney

Serve these golden spiced potatoes with chilled yogurt sprinkled with chopped fresh cilantro leaves, and some mango chutney.

1 Cook the potatoes in boiling salted water until they are just tender but still firm. Drain well, then set aside to cool. When cool, cut them into dice.

2 Heat the oil in a large skillet and add the chili, garlic, cumin, and mustard seeds. Fry for 2–3 minutes, without browning the garlic, until the spices release their aroma.

3 Stir in the turmeric, salt, and chili powder, and then add the diced potatoes. Fry gently over moderate heat until the potatoes are crisp, golden brown, heated through, and coated with spices.

4 Serve the spiced potatoes very hot with some yogurt, sprinkled with cilantro, and mango chutney.

Serves 4–6

Green Beans with Chilies

Rosti Potato Cakes

Rosti is a traditional Swiss way of cooking potatoes. Here, instead of preparing a large dish of rosti, the grated potato is made into little crisp, golden-brown fritters.

2 pounds potatoes
3 eggs, beaten
1 onion, grated
1 garlic clove, minced
1 tablespoon flour
2 tablespoons chopped
parsley and chives
pinch of grated nutmeg
sea salt and freshly ground black
pepper
corn oil for frying

1 Peel the potatoes and grate them coarsely with a grater or in a food processor. Put the grated potato in a sieve and rinse under running cold water. Drain well and then pat dry with paper towels.

2 Put the grated potato in a large mixing bowl with the beaten eggs, and mix well together. Stir in the grated onion, minced garlic, flour, chopped herbs, and nutmeg. Season with salt and pepper.

3 Divide the potato mixture into 12–16 equal-sized portions, and then shape them into small rounds with your hands.

4 Heat the oil in a skillet and fry the potato cakes, a few at a time, until crisp and golden brown on both sides—turn them halfway through cooking. Drain on paper towels, and serve very hot.

Serves 4–6

Stir-fried Mushrooms

You can use either large white mushrooms or a mixture of different mushrooms in this traditional Chinese dish. Try some Oriental shiitake and oyster mushrooms.

4 tablespoons corn or
peanut oil
4 scallions,
finely chopped
2 garlic cloves, minced
3 cups washed and shredded dark
cabbage
1 pound mushrooms,
quartered or sliced
1 teaspoon chili bean sauce or chili
powder (optional)
2 tablespoons dark soy sauce
1 tablespoon rice wine
or dry sherry
pinch of sugar
salt and freshly ground
black pepper
1 tablespoon chopped fresh
cilantro leaves

1 Heat the oil in a wok or a deep skillet. When it is hot, throw in the scallions and garlic and stir-fry for about 2 minutes.

2 Stir in the shredded cabbage and cook briskly, turning it in the oil until it goes bright green. Add the mushrooms and continue stir-frying for 2–3 minutes.

3 Add the chili bean sauce or chili powder (if using) together with the soy sauce, rice wine or sherry, and a pinch of sugar. Continue stir-frying for a few more minutes until the liquid evaporates and the mushrooms are tender. Check the seasoning before adding salt and pepper. Sprinkle with chopped cilantro and serve immediately.

Serves 4

Caramelized **Onions**

Use small pearl onions in this dish and keep a close eye on them while they are cooking to insure that they do not burn. Serve with Cheese and Potato Fritters or Beanburgers.

1 pound pearl onions
1 tablespoon sugar
1 tablespoon butter
salt and freshly ground
black pepper

1 Peel the onions and arrange in a single layer in a large skillet. Sprinkle with sugar, dot with butter, and barely cover with cold water.

2 Cover the skillet and bring to a boil, and then uncover and cook vigorously until the liquid evaporates and the onions are coated in a golden brown syrup. Watch them closely when the sugar starts to caramelize

and shake the skillet to turn the onions in the syrup. Season with salt and pepper and serve immediately.

Serves 4

Roasted onions

This is a good way of serving larger onions. Peel the onions and put them in a roasting pan. Brush them generously with olive oil and melted butter, and bake in a preheated oven at 350°F for about 45 minutes. Serve sprinkled with a dusting of sea salt.

Leeks in Parsley Sauce

This is a wonderful way of serving leeks, or fava beans, carrots, or broccoli for that matter. The sauce should be light and creamy, barely coating rather than drowning the leeks.

2 pounds leeks, washed, trimmed,
and roughly chopped

FOR THE SAUCE:
1¼ cups milk
1 onion stuck with 2 cloves
bouquet garni
salt and freshly ground
black pepper
2 tablespoons butter
2 tablespoons flour
small bunch parsley,
finely chopped
⅝ cup heavy cream
squeeze of lemon juice

1 Make the sauce. Put the milk, onion, and bouquet garni in a saucepan with a little salt and pepper and bring to the boil. Reduce the heat to the barest simmer, and heat through very gently for 30 minutes. Strain, reserving the flavored milk.

2 Melt the butter in a pan and stir in the flour. Cook for 2 minutes, without browning, then gradually

beat in the flavored milk, until you have a smooth, thick sauce. Cook very gently over low heat for 10–15 minutes. Season to taste and stir in the parsley and cream.

3 Meanwhile, cook the leeks in lightly salted boiling water for 3–4 minutes, until they are just tender. Drain well. Stir the leeks into the hot parsley sauce, then add a squeeze of lemon juice and transfer to a serving dish.

Serves 4

Fruity Red Cabbage

Red cabbage can be cooked with many winter fruits, including apples, pears, juniper berries, and cranberries. Unlike most other vegetables, it can be cooked in advance and actually tastes even better when it has been reheated.

2 tablespoons peanut or corn oil
1 onion, finely chopped
8 juniper berries, crushed
2 green apples, peeled, cored, and diced
1 cup cranberries
5 cups shredded red cabbage
pinch of ground cinnamon
pinch of ground allspice
pinch of grated nutmeg
1 tablespoon brown sugar
1/2 cup red wine
1 tablespoon red wine vinegar
salt and freshly ground black pepper
1 tablespoon cranberry jelly (optional)

1 Heat the oil in a large flameproof casserole dish, and gently fry the onion until soft and golden. Add the crushed juniper berries, diced apples, and cranberries, and cook gently for 2–3 minutes.

2 Stir in the red cabbage, spices, sugar, wine, and wine vinegar. Stir well, then cover the casserole dish and cook in a preheated moderate oven at 350°F for about 1 hour, or until the cabbage is tender. Season to taste with salt and pepper, and, if wished, stir in the cranberry jelly.

Serves 4-6

Barbecued Salad

1/2 pound thin asparagus stalks, trimmed
1 red bell pepper, seeded and cut into thick strips
1 yellow bell pepper, seeded and cut into thick strips
8 scallions, trimmed
1 radicchio, trimmed and cut into wedges
oil for brushing
small bunch of arugula
1/2 pound baby spinach leaves
salt and freshly ground black pepper

FOR THE DRESSING:
4 tablespoons fruity green olive oil
1 tablespoon balsamic vinegar
squeeze of lime juice
pinch of sugar
1 tablespoon chopped basil
1 tablespoon chopped fresh cilantro leaves

This may sound bizarre, but it is a brilliant colorful salad with a distinctive smoky flavor. The vegetables and salad leaves are seared quickly on a grill over hot coals, tossed in a herb vinaigrette and eaten warm. It is characteristic of the new healthy and thoughtful style of Californian cooking.

1 Cook the asparagus in salted boiling water for 4–5 minutes. Drain well. Brush the bell peppers and scallions with olive oil and place on a grill over hot coals. Grill quickly, turning frequently and brushing with more oil if necessary, until the vegetables are just starting to char.

2 Brush the radicchio with oil and grill for 1–2 minutes each side, with the asparagus. Toss the arugula and baby spinach leaves on the grill—just long enough to wilt them.

3 Mix all the dressing ingredients together and toss the barbecued vegetables lightly in the herb dressing. Season with salt and pepper, and serve warm.

Serves 4

Leeks Niçoise

This warm leek salad is popular throughout France, but in Provence it is served with black olives and hard-boiled eggs. Use slim leeks rather than fat ones. You can serve thin green beans or asparagus in the same way.

1½ pounds slim leeks
2 hard-boiled eggs, peeled and chopped
1 tablespoon chopped parsley
½ cup black olives, pitted

FOR THE DRESSING:
½ cup extra-virgin olive oil
2 tablespoons white wine vinegar
2 teaspoons Dijon mustard
½ teaspoon sugar
salt and freshly ground black pepper

1 Trim the leeks, removing the dark green leaves. Wash them thoroughly under running cold water to remove any mud. Pat dry with paper towels.

2 Cook the leeks in salted boiling water for 8–10 minutes, until just cooked and tender. Drain well and dry on paper towels.

3 While the leeks are cooking, make the dressing. Mix the olive oil and wine vinegar, then stir in the Dijon mustard and sugar until smooth. Season with salt and pepper.

4 Arrange the warm leeks in a serving dish and pour the dressing over the top. Sprinkle the chopped egg over the leeks and scatter with parsley. Serve the leeks warm with some black olives.

Serves 4–6

Leeks Niçoise

Christmas **Salad**

A fresh-tasting salad makes a welcome change at Christmas after all the rich food. This salad uses seasonal winter leaves and fresh fruit and cheese.

2 heads chicory
1 radicchio (red chicory)
1 red onion, finely chopped
2 red apples, cored and cubed
1/2 cup coarsely chopped walnuts
4 ounces blue cheese, cubed
1 avocado, pitted, and thinly sliced

3 tablespoons chopped parsley and chives

FOR THE DRESSING:
4 tablespoons olive oil
1 tablespoon red wine vinegar
freshly ground black pepper

1 Wash and trim the chicory and radicchio, and separate them into leaves. Arrange in a salad bowl with the red onion, apples, walnuts, blue cheese, and avocado.

2 Mix the dressing ingredients together and then toss the salad gently until everything is glistening with oil. Sprinkle the chopped parsley and chives over the top and serve immediately.

Serves 4–6

Greek **Bean** Salad

Cannellini or white beans can be substituted for black-eyed peas in this classic Greek salad of Romaine lettuce and feta cheese.

1 1/3 cups dried black-eyed peas
1 red onion, thinly sliced
4 ripe tomatoes, quartered
leaves of 1 Romaine lettuce
1/2 cup black olives, pitted
6 ounces feta cheese, cubed
1 tablespoon chopped chives
1 tablespoon chopped fresh cilantro

FOR THE DRESSING:
4 tablespoons fruity green Greek olive oil
juice of 1/2 lemon
1 garlic clove, minced (optional)
pinch of sugar
salt and freshly ground black pepper

1 Soak the black-eyed peas in some cold water overnight. Drain, rinse under running cold water and put the beans in a saucepan. Cover with fresh water and bring to the boil. Reduce the heat and cook gently for about 1 hour, until the beans are tender but not mushy. Drain well.

2 Mix the beans with the red onion, tomatoes, and Romaine lettuce in a large salad bowl. Mix the dressing ingredients together and gently toss the bean salad.

3 Scatter the olives, feta cheese, chopped chives, and cilantro over the bean salad, and serve.

Serves 4–6

Caesar Salad with Grilled **Goat's Cheese**

leaves of 1 head Romaine lettuce
6 ounces round chèvre (goat's cheese), cut into 4 slices

FOR THE DRESSING:
2 eggs
1/2 cup fruity olive oil
juice of 1 lemon
dash of Worcestershire sauce
1/3 cup freshly grated vegetarian Parmesan cheese
salt and freshly ground black pepper

FOR THE GARLIC CROUTONS:
4 thick slices crusty white bread
2 tablespoons olive oil
2 garlic cloves, minced

This salad tastes fantastic with garlic croutons and grilled goat's cheese. You could also top it with slices of grilled tofu (bean curd).

1 Make the garlic croutons: remove the crusts from the bread and cut into dice. Put the olive oil and garlic in a bowl and toss the bread in it. Put the croutons on a cookie sheet and cook in a preheated oven at 350°F for 5–10 minutes, until crisp and golden. Set the garlic croutons aside to cool.

2 Make the dressing: boil the eggs in their shells for 1 minute and then run some cold water over them. Break the eggs into a bowl and beat well. Beat in the olive oil slowly in a thin, steady stream. Stir in the lemon juice, Worcestershire sauce, Parmesan cheese, and seasoning.

3 Put the Romaine lettuce in a large salad bowl and toss in the dressing. Add the garlic croutons and toss again. Divide the Caesar Salad between 4 serving plates.

4 Quickly grill or broil the slices of goat's cheese until softened and just starting to ooze and turn brown. Arrange them on top of the salad and serve immediately.

Serves 4

Celeriac Salads

More good winter salads for when you are getting fed up with the usual seasonal hot root vegetables. If you can't obtain celeriac, substitute turnips, chayote, or celery instead.

1 Trim and peel the celeriac and cut into julienne (matchstick) strips, dropping them into a bowl of cold water and lemon juice.

2 Bring a saucepan of water to a boil and then add the celeriac. Return to a boil and cook for 1 minute, then drain and rinse under running cold water. Pat dry with paper towels or a clean cloth.

3 Now prepare one of the salads. For the vinaigrette, mix the celeriac with

1 large celeriac
juice of 1 lemon

FOR THE VINAIGRETTE SALAD:
2–3 apples, cored and diced
1/2 cup chopped walnuts
3 tablespoons olive or walnut oil
1 tablespoon white wine vinegar
salt and freshly ground black pepper

1 tablespoon finely chopped parsley

FOR THE MUSTARDY SALAD:
5/8 cup mayonnaise
5/8 cup fromage frais
2 teaspoons whole-grain or Dijon mustard
squeeze of lemon juice
salt and freshly ground black pepper
1 tablespoon finely chopped parsley

the apples and walnuts in a bowl. Blend the oil, wine vinegar, and seasoning and pour over the celeriac mixture. Toss gently together, sprinkle with parsley and serve.

4 For the mustardy salad, mix together the mayonnaise (homemade if possible) with the fromage frais, mustard, and lemon juice. Season to taste, then stir in the partly cooked strips of celeriac. Sprinkle with parsley and serve.

Serves 4

Warm **Potato** Vinaigrette

At any time of year, this warm potato salad is a welcome addition to a meal. Use red-skinned or waxy new potatoes if possible. Many food markets now sell special potato varieties for salads.

1¹/₂ pounds small potatoes, washed
but not peeled
1 bunch scallions, chopped
3 tablespoons chopped fresh chives

FOR THE DRESSING:
4 tablespoons extra-virgin olive oil
1 tablespoon white wine vinegar
salt and freshly ground
black pepper

1 Cook the potatoes in lightly salted boiling water until tender but not mushy. Drain well and cut in half or into smaller pieces.

2 Mix the potatoes with the scallions. Mix the dressing ingredients together and pour over the potatoes and onions. Toss lightly, sprinkle with chives and serve warm.

Serves 4

Variations

1 Instead of chives, add a mixture of chopped summer herbs, e.g., mint, oregano, and tarragon.

2 Mix the warm potatoes with chopped fresh red chili, chopped red onion, and fresh cilantro, then toss in the vinaigrette.

3 Substitute crème fraîche or sour cream for the vinaigrette dressing, and sprinkle with plenty of chopped chives.

Warm Spinach Salad

Warm **Spinach** Salad

You must use young tender baby spinach leaves for this salad, not the older, larger leaves which can be very fibrous with tough stems. It can be served as a first course or even as a light meal if you add cherry tomatoes, sliced avocado, hard-boiled eggs, and mozzarella, feta, or goat's cheese. Or serve with hard-boiled eggs.

2 red bell peppers
1/2 cup extra-virgin olive oil
12 ounces mushrooms, e.g., cèpes, chanterelles, morels
3 tablespoons balsamic vinegar
pinch of sugar
salt and freshly ground black pepper
1/2 pound baby spinach leaves
1/2 cup chopped walnuts
1 tablespoon chopped parsley

1 Put the red bell peppers under a preheated hot broiler, and broil, turning occasionally, until the skins are blistered and charred. Place the peppers in a plastic bag until cool, then peel off the skins, remove the seeds, and cut into thin strips.

2 Heat 4 tablespoons of the olive oil in a small skillet, and add the mushrooms. Fry gently for about 5 minutes, until cooked. Add 2 tablespoons of the balsamic vinegar and a good pinch of sugar, and continue cooking for 1 minute. Season to taste with salt and pepper and set aside while you quickly prepare the spinach salad.

3 Wash and dry the spinach leaves and put them in a bowl with the walnuts. Mix the remaining olive oil and balsamic vinegar and use to toss the spinach.

4 Divide the dressed spinach and walnuts between 4 plates and arrange the warm mushrooms and their juices, and the broiled red bell pepper strips on top. Sprinkle with chopped parsley and serve.

Serves 4

Crunchy **Carrot** Salad

This is a great winter salad, which is especially good at Christmas. As an alternative, you can mix the vegetables, fruit, and nuts with some mayonnaise and fromage frais, and use it as a topping for baked potatoes.

4 large carrots
2 sticks celery
1 small onion
2 red apples
1/3 cup raisins
1/2 cup chopped hazelnuts or almonds
2 tablespoons sesame seeds

1 tablespoon chopped chives
2 tablespoons chopped parsley

FOR THE DRESSING:
5 tablespoons olive oil
juice of 1/2 lemon
pinch of sugar
salt and freshly ground black pepper

1 Peel the carrots and cut them into matchstick-sized sticks. Trim the celery and cut into dice. Peel and grate the onion. Cut the apples in half, scoop out the cores, and cut the flesh into dice.

2 Put the carrots, celery, onion, and apples in a large bowl with the raisins, chopped nuts, and sesame seeds, and mix well.

3 Mix all the dressing ingredients together and pour over the carrot mixture. Toss gently so everything is coated with the dressing, then chill in the refrigerator for at least 30 minutes.

4 Serve the carrot salad, sprinkled with chopped chives and parsley.

Serves 4

Mexican Baja **Salad**

This is typical of the new breed of salads eaten on the Baja peninsula and on the West Coast of the United States. Serve it with tacos, burritos, and other Mexican or Tex-Mex dishes.

3 ounces Romaine lettuce
3 ounces curly endive (frisée)
3 ounces arugula
1 small radicchio (red chicory)
1 large carrot
1 zucchini, diced or thinly sliced
1 red bell pepper, seeded and chopped
1 red onion, finely chopped
6-8 cherry tomatoes, halved
small bunch of chives, chopped
few cilantro leaves, coarsely chopped

FOR THE DRESSING:
1 avocado, peeled and pitted
4 tablespoons olive oil
1 tablespoon wine vinegar
squeeze of lime juice
1 fat garlic clove, minced
freshly ground black pepper

1 Wash the salad leaves thoroughly and spin dry. Separate the radicchio into leaves, then wash well and dry. Place all the salad leaves in a large salad bowl.

2 Peel the carrot and then, using the same potato peeler, peel off long strips. Add to the salad leaves with the zucchini, red bell pepper, red onion, and cherry tomatoes.

3 Make the dressing. Mash the avocado flesh with a fork, and then beat in the olive oil, wine vinegar, lime juice, and garlic until well blended. If the dressing is too thick, add a little more olive oil. Season with plenty of freshly ground black pepper.

4 Toss the salad gently in the dressing and sprinkle with chopped chives and chopped cilantro. Serve the salad immediately before the dressing starts to discolor.

Serves 4–6

Spanish **Roasted Vegetable** Salad

This Catalan specialty is better known in Spain as *escalivada*. The vegetables can be roasted in the oven or, if you prefer a smoky, slightly charred flavor, cooked on a grill over hot coals. You can eat this salad either warm or cold.

1 large eggplant
1 red bell pepper
1 green bell pepper
2 Spanish onions
2 zucchini
6 fat garlic cloves, unpeeled
sprigs of fresh thyme and rosemary
6 tablespoons olive oil
sea salt and freshly ground black pepper
4 ripe tomatoes
2 tablespoons sherry vinegar
juice of 1/2 lemon
2 tablespoons chopped parsley

1 Place the eggplant, red and green bell peppers, onions, and zucchini in a large roasting pan. Tuck the garlic cloves and sprigs of fresh thyme and rosemary into the gaps between the vegetables.

2 Sprinkle the olive oil over all the vegetables and season with salt and pepper. Bake the vegetables in a preheated oven at 350°F for 30–40 minutes, adding the tomatoes after 15 minutes.

3 Let the vegetables cool a little, then slice the eggplant and zucchini thickly, and seed and slice the bell peppers. Cut the onions into wedges, and halve or quarter the tomatoes. Arrange all the vegetables on a large serving platter.

4 Peel the roasted garlic cloves and mash the flesh into the olive oil pan juices. Mix in the sherry vinegar and lemon juice, and pour over the roasted vegetables. Sprinkle with chopped parsley and serve with crusty bread to mop up the delicious garlic dressing on the plates.

Serves 4–6

Greek Country **Salad**

The addition of salty feta cheese turns a fresh rustic salad into a light lunch for summer. Serve with hard-boiled eggs and some crusty bread. You could grill some bell peppers and eggplants until slightly charred, and then slice them over the salad.

1 head Romaine lettuce
1/2 cucumber, sliced thinly
4 large ripe tomatoes, skinned and quartered
bunch of scallions, trimmed and sliced
6 sprigs of fresh mint, chopped
1 tablespoon chopped fresh oregano
2 tablespoons chopped parsley or cilantro leaves
8 ounces feta cheese, cubed
1/2 cup black olives
lemon quarters, to serve

FOR THE DRESSING:
5 tablespoons fruity green olive oil
juice of 1 lemon
pinch of sugar
salt and freshly ground black pepper

1 Wash the lettuce, trim the base, and separate the leaves. Dry them thoroughly, then shred the leaves and place them in a large salad bowl.

2 Add the cucumber, tomatoes, scallions, and chopped herbs to the lettuce in the bowl, and toss together lightly.

3 Blend the olive oil and lemon juice for the dressing with the sugar, and season with salt and pepper. Pour over the salad and toss gently.

4 Scatter the feta cheese over the salad and serve with black olives and lemon quarters.

Serves 4

Goat's Cheese and Puy Lentil Salad

If you can't get the tiny greenish-black Puy lentils for this warm winter salad, you can use brown lentils instead.

1 1/3 cups Puy lentils
1 bay leaf
8 cherry tomatoes, halved
2 ounces watercress or arugula
6 ounces goat's cheese, cubed
1 tablespoon chopped parsley
1 tablespoon chopped chives

FOR THE DRESSING:
6 tablespoons extra-virgin olive oil
2 tablespoons lemon juice
1/2 teaspoon Dijon mustard
salt and freshly ground black pepper

1 Put the lentils in a strainer and wash them under running cold water. Drain and put the lentils into a saucepan. Add the bay leaf and cover with plenty of cold water. Bring to a boil and continue boiling for 15–20 minutes, until the lentils are cooked and tender. Drain them in a colander.

2 Mix the warm lentils with the cherry tomatoes, watercress or arugula, and goat's cheese in a large salad bowl.

3 Make the dressing: blend the olive oil, lemon juice, and mustard, and season with salt and pepper to taste. Toss the lentil salad in the dressing, sprinkle with chopped parsley and chives, and serve immediately while the salad is still warm.

Serves 4

Winter **Venetian** Salad

2 red bell peppers
2 radicchios (red chicory)
1 bunch red leaf lettuce
1 bunch arugula leaves
small bunch watercress
mozzarella cheese, to serve
freshly ground black pepper

FOR THE DRESSING:
4 tablespoons extra-virgin olive oil
1 tablespoon balsamic vinegar
juice of ¹/2 lemon

Colorful salads of radicchio and crisp bitter leaves are popular in Venice, where they are eaten in a simple dressing of olive oil, vinegar, and lemon juice.

1 Put the red bell peppers under a preheated hot broiler, turning them occasionally, until the skins are blistered and charred all over. Remove the bell peppers and place in a plastic bag. When cool, remove the skins and seeds, and cut the bell peppers into strips.

2 Blend the olive oil with the balsamic vinegar and lemon juice. Put all the salad leaves in a bowl and toss in the dressing. Scatter the grilled red bell pepper strips over the top. Serve with mozzarella cheese dressed with a little olive oil and sprinkled with freshly ground black pepper.

Serves 4

Satay Salad

This Thai salad combines warm vegetables in a spicy dressing flavored with coconut milk, curry paste, and peanuts. You can buy a hot curry paste if you don't want to make it yourself.

3 carrots, peeled and cut into matchstick strips
1¹/2 cups shredded cabbage
¹/4 pound thin green beans, trimmed
1 red bell pepper, seeded and sliced
1 green bell pepper, seeded and sliced
¹/4 pound bean sprouts
4 ounces canned water chestnuts, drained and sliced
2 tablespoons chopped fresh cilantro leaves

FOR THE DRESSING:
2 tablespoons peanut oil
1 tablespoon curry paste
1¹/4 cups coconut milk
2 tablespoons soy sauce
2 teaspoons brown sugar
1 teaspoon ground coriander
2 teaspoons ground cumin
juice of 1 lime
3 tablespoons crushed roasted peanuts or peanut butter
salt and freshly ground black pepper

Hot curry paste

1-inch piece fresh ginger root, peeled and chopped
4 fresh red chilies, seeded and chopped
1 stalk lemon grass, chopped
1 small onion, finely chopped
2 garlic cloves, minced
1 teaspoon coriander seeds
¹/2 teaspoon ground cumin
juice of ¹/2 lime
3 tablespoons chopped cilantro leaves
salt and ground black pepper

Put all the ingredients in a food processor or blender, and process to a paste. Store in a sealed jar in the refrigerator for up to one week. Use in Thai vegetable curries and stir-fries.

1 Cook the carrots, cabbage, green beans and peppers in boiling water for 3–4 minutes, until just tender but still crisp. Drain well and mix with the bean sprouts and water chestnuts in a large salad bowl.

2 Heat the peanut oil and stir in the curry paste. Cook gently for 1 minute, then add the coconut milk, soy sauce, brown sugar, spices, and lime juice. Stir in the peanuts and simmer gently for 3–4 minutes. Season.

3 Remove from the heat, allow to cool a little and then pour the warm dressing over the vegetables and toss well. Serve warm, sprinkled with cilantro.

Serves 4

Moroccan **Orange** Salad

4 large oranges
¹/4 pound baby spinach leaves,
arugula, or watercress
1 cup small black olives
grated rind and juice of 1 orange
3 tablespoons olive oil
dash of white wine vinegar
salt and freshly ground
black pepper
chopped fresh cilantro leaves,
to garnish

Oranges are often made into a salad with salt and olives in North Africa and southern Italy. Serve it on a bed of young spinach leaves or some bitter, pungent arugula and watercress.

1 Peel the oranges with a sharp knife, removing all the white pith, then cut the flesh horizontally into thin slices.

2 Arrange the orange slices on top of the spinach, arugula, or watercress, and scatter with the black olives.

3 Mix the grated orange rind and juice with the olive oil and a dash of wine vinegar. Pour over the orange salad and season to taste with salt and pepper. Sprinkle with chopped cilantro and serve at once.

Serves 4

Lentil and Tomato Salad

Lentils tossed in vinaigrette make an earthy, filling summer salad. Serve it as a main course with hard-boiled eggs and crusty buttered wholemeal bread.

1¹/3 cups brown Continental lentils
1 red onion, finely chopped
4 scallions, finely chopped
4 ripe tomatoes, quartered
5 tablespoons fruity green
olive oil

1 tablespoon red wine vinegar
pinch of sugar
salt and freshly ground
black pepper
2 tablespoons chopped parsley
and mint

1 Put the lentils in a bowl, cover with cold water and leave to soak for 1 hour. Remove any gritty pieces that float to the surface, then drain the lentils in a sieve.

2 Place them in a saucepan, cover with fresh water and cook for about

1¹/4 hours, or until tender. Drain the lentils well and then mix in a large bowl with the red onion, scallions, and quartered tomatoes.

3 Blend the olive oil, wine vinegar, and sugar together, and pour over

the lentils, onions, and tomatoes. Toss gently and season with salt and plenty of black pepper. Sprinkle with the chopped parsley and mint, and serve.

Serves 4

Desserts

Here's a selection of hot, comforting desserts for cold days, and fruity, refreshing desserts, and ice creams and sorbets for hot weather. What they all have in common is seasonal fruits—juicy fruits and berries in summer; apples, pears, and orchard fruits in the fall; and dried fruits and citrus fruits in winter. Always try to use organic, unblemished fruit and organic cereals and flour in order to obtain the best and most healthy results. Fresh ingredients of the highest quality make all the difference when it comes to creating delicious desserts—do not be tempted to cheat.

Tropical **Fruit** Kebabs

4 small bananas
1 large mango
1 ripe papaya (pawpaw)
¹/₂ fresh pineapple
4 peaches
¹/₄ cup sugar
3 tablespoons dark rum
powdered sugar, for dusting

FOR THE CHOCOLATE SAUCE:
5 ounces semisweet chocolate
¹/₂ cup heavy cream

FOR THE FRUIT MASCARPONE:
4 ounces ripe strawberries
1 tablespoon sugar
¹/₂ cup mascarpone cheese

Serve these kebabs with a decadently rich hot sauce of melted bitter chocolate. Alternatively, mash some strawberries or raspberries into a bowl of mascarpone cheese and put a spoonful on each dessert plate.

1 Peel the bananas and cut into quarters. Peel and pit the mango and cut the flesh into large chunks. Peel the papaya, remove the seeds, and cut into chunks. Remove the peel from the pineapple and slice thickly. Discard the central core, and cut each slice into large chunks. Pit and quarter the peaches.

2 Thread the fruit alternately on to wooden skewers. Sprinkle generously with sugar and then place under a preheated hot broiler for about 5 minutes. Turn the fruit kebabs frequently so that they caramelize evenly.

3 Meanwhile, make the chocolate sauce: break the chocolate into a basin and set over a saucepan of simmering water until melted. Bring the cream to the boil, and stir into the melted chocolate.

4 Mash the strawberries, sweeten with sugar, and then stir into the mascarpone cheese.

5 Heat the rum, set it alight and pour it flaming over the fruit kebabs. Serve immediately, dusted with powdered sugar, with the chocolate sauce and strawberry mascarpone.

Serves 4

Other fruit kebabs

1 Thread peeled and quartered apples on to skewers, brush with lemon juice and then with melted butter and sugar. Broil until caramelized and serve with crème fraîche.

2 Thread quartered bananas on to skewers, brush with lemon juice, sprinkle with sugar, and broil. Make a toffee sauce by heating 1 stick butter and ¹/₂ cup brown sugar with a good pinch each of cinnamon and nutmeg. Whisk in ⁵/₈ cup heavy cream.

Tropical Fruit Kebabs

Quick Fruit **Brulée**

1¼ pounds mixed fruits
1¼ cups heavy cream
³/4 cup sugar

Make this dessert at any time of the year, adding a variety of seasonal fruits: soft berry fruits (raspberries and strawberries), peaches, apricots, or plums in the summer; sliced bananas, grapes, oranges, poached apples, or pears in the winter.

1 Prepare the fruits, removing any pits, stalks, etc., and, if large, cut into smaller pieces. Place all the fruits in a large serving dish or, if wished, arrange them in the bases of 4 individual dishes.

2 Beat the cream until it is thick and stands up in soft peaks. Spoon it over the fruits to completely cover them and level the top. Chill in the refrigerator for at least 15 minutes.

3 Put the sugar in a heavy-based saucepan with 4 tablespoons of cold water. Stir over gentle heat until the sugar dissolves. Turn up the heat and boil hard until the sugar syrup turns golden. Keep an eye on it so that as soon as it caramelizes and turns golden brown you can remove it from the heat before it burns.

4 Carefully pour the caramel over the top of the whipped cream to cover it evenly. You must do this immediately. Leave to cool for a few minutes before serving.

Serves 4

Summer Fruit **Tarts**

It's not time consuming to make delicious little tarts if you cheat and use ready made puff pastry. Buy it freshly made or frozen. Top the tarts with different fruits of varying colors, such as plums, apricots, peaches, apples, cherries, and soft berry fruits.

12 ounces puff pastry
1 pound mixed
summer fruits
sugar, for sprinkling
3 tablespoons apricot jam
1 tablespoon water
squeeze of lemon juice

1 Roll out the puff pastry on a lightly floured surface and cut into rounds, about 3 inches in diameter.

2 Arrange the summer fruits on top of the rounds of pastry. Use pitted and sliced peaches or nectarines; halved and stoned small apricots or plums; pitted cherries or any other soft berry fruits. Sprinkle the fruit lightly with a little sugar.

3 Bake in a preheated oven at 425°F for about 15 minutes, until the pastry has risen and is golden, and the fruit is cooked and tender.

4 Heat the apricot jam with the water and lemon juice, and stir well. Brush the tarts lightly with the apricot glaze and serve warm with a bowl of heavy cream.

Serves 4–6

Spanish Orange **Rice**

Cold and creamy rice desserts, perfumed with orange, are eaten throughout Spain and Mexico. Serve as a chilled summer dessert in a pool of fresh fruit coulis or with a fruit compôte.

1½ cups milk
freshly pared rind of 1 orange
¼ cup sugar
¼ cup short-grain rice, rinsed
2 egg yolks
juice of 1 orange

FOR THE CARAMEL:
¼ cup sugar
3 tablespoons water

1 Put the milk and orange rind in a saucepan with the sugar. Heat gently, stirring until the sugar dissolves. Bring to a boil, then stir in the rice and simmer gently for 25–30 minutes, until the rice mixture is thickened and creamy.

2 Discard the strips of orange rind. Beat the egg yolks into the creamy rice mixture and then stir in the orange juice.

3 Put the sugar and water for the caramel in a small saucepan. Stir over low heat until the sugar dissolves, and then bring to a boil. Cook rapidly over high heat until it turns a rich golden brown. Pour the caramel into 6 small molds, tilting each one to coat the base and sides.

4 Fill the molds with the rice mixture and stand them in a roasting pan. Pour in enough warm water to come halfway up the sides of the molds. Cook the rice in a preheated oven at 350°F for 20–25 minutes.

5 Remove the molds from the oven and set aside to cool, then chill in the refrigerator until ready to serve. Turn out the molds and serve the rice puddings with fresh apricot coulis (sweetened sieved apricots) or a fruit compôte of summer berries.

Serves 4

Poached **Pears** in Beaumes de Venise

This makes a wonderful winter dessert—light and refreshing. Serve hot with crème fraîche, vanilla ice cream, or some thick plain yogurt.

1¼ cups Beaumes de Venise wine
1¼ cups water
½ cup sugar
thinly pared lemon rind

1 vanilla bean
1 cinnamon stick
6 dessert pears, firm but ripe
crème fraîche, to serve

1 Pour the wine and water into a large saucepan. Add the sugar, lemon rind, vanilla bean, and cinnamon stick. Stir gently over low heat until the sugar dissolves.

2 Peel the pears, cut them in half, and carefully cut out the cores. Place the halved pears in the liquid in the saucepan and turn up the heat to simmering point. Cover the pan and simmer gently for 10–15 minutes, until the pears are tender.

3 Remove the pears with a slotted spoon and place them in a serving dish. Return the poaching liquid to the heat and bring to a boil. Boil until it reduces by at least half. Remove the vanilla bean and cinnamon stick, and then pour the syrup over the pears. Cool and then chill before serving with crème fraîche.

Serves 4

Strawberry Hazelnut Meringue

A dessert to die for on a hot, sultry summer's day—juicy ripe strawberries and thick cream sandwiched in crisp nutty meringue. It tastes equally good with raspberries or cherries.

1 Break the egg whites into a large bowl and beat until stiff. Gradually beat in the sugar, a spoonful at a time, and, lastly, the vinegar. Gently fold the toasted chopped hazelnuts into the meringue.

4 egg whites
1 cup sugar
$^1/_2$ teaspoon vinegar
$^1/_2$ cup toasted hazelnuts, finely chopped
$1^1/_4$ cups heavy cream
8 ounces strawberries
powdered sugar, for dusting

2 Line two 7-inch layer cake pans with parchment paper, and divide the meringue between the pans. Bake in a preheated oven at 250°F for about $1^1/_4$ hours, until the meringue is crisp and firm.

3 Leave in the pans until cold and then turn out the meringues. Beat the cream until stiff and then spread it over the meringues. Scatter the strawberries over the meringue base and dust with powdered sugar. Place the other meringue on top and dust with more sugar. Chill in the refrigerator before serving.

Serves 6

Winter Fruit Compôte

3 cups mixed no-soak dried fruit, e.g., apricots, figs, peaches, prunes
$^1/_3$ cup raisins
juice of 2 oranges
1 cinnamon stick
$1^1/_4$ cups water
$1^1/_4$ cups port or sweet wine
2 tablespoons pistachio nuts

A compôte of dried fruits can be served chilled or warm with cream or vanilla ice cream. It makes a particularly welcome change at Christmas after all the rich meals. If you have a sweet tooth, you can sweeten it with a little brown sugar or honey.

1 Put the mixed dried fruit and raisins in a saucepan with the orange juice, cinnamon stick, and water. Cover the pan and simmer gently over low heat for 20 minutes.

2 Remove from the heat and add the port or wine and pistachio nuts. Leave to cool, then pour into a large serving bowl and chill in the refrigerator for several hours. Serve chilled or warm with crème fraîche or vanilla ice cream.

Serves 4

Opposite: Winter Fruit Compôte

Pear frangipane tart

Serves 6

This mouthwatering tart is usually made with pears or apples. Make sure that the pears are not under-ripe, or they will not cook to a succulent softness but will remain hard. In summer, you can substitute poached apricots, peaches, or cherries.

8 tablespoons butter
¹/₂ cup sugar
2 eggs
1 cup ground almonds
1 tablespoon all-purpose flour
3 large pears, ripe but firm

FOR THE PIE CRUST:
2 cups all-purpose flour
pinch of salt

1 stick butter, cut into dice
1 tablespoon vanilla sugar
1 large egg yolk
cold water, for mixing

FOR THE APRICOT GLAZE:
¹/₄ cup apricot jam
2 tablespoons water
1 teaspoon lemon juice

1 Make the pie crust dough: sift the flour and salt into a bowl and rub in the butter until the mixture looks like fine bread crumbs. Add the vanilla sugar, and then bind together with the egg yolk and a little cold water, if necessary. Chill in the refrigerator for 30 minutes. Roll out the dough and use to line a well-buttered 10-inch springform pie pan. Chill in the refrigerator while you make the filling.

2 Cream the butter and sugar together, then beat in the eggs, one at a time. Beat in the ground almonds and flour. Spread over the base of the prepared pie crust shell.

3 Peel and halve the pears, carefully removing the cores. Slice each half

through thinly at a slight angle, keeping it intact, and then arrange the sliced pear halves in a circle, like the spokes of a wheel, on top of the frangipane filling. Bake in a hot preheated oven at 400°F for 15 minutes, then reduce the oven temperature to 325°F and bake for a further 15 minutes, until the frangipane filling is firm and golden, and the pie crust is crisp. Cool.

4 Make the apricot glaze: heat the apricot jam with the water and lemon juice, and pass through a strainer. When the tart is just warm, remove it from the pan and lightly brush the top of the frangipane and the pears with the apricot glaze. Serve warm with crème fraîche or heavy cream.

Variations

1 Summer fruits include poached apricots, cherries, peaches, and raspberries.

2 Winter fruits include apples, blackberries, mango, and kiwi fruit.

Strawberry Zabaglione

In Italy, zabaglione is always served hot straight from the pan, but add some strawberries and cream, and it makes a delicious iced dessert.

1¼ cups heavy cream
4 egg yolks
5 tablespoons sugar
8 tablespoons Marsala
2 cups strawberries
sprigs of mint, for decoration

1 Beat the heavy cream until stiff, then cover and chill throughly in the refrigerator.

2 Put the egg yolks and sugar in the top of a double-boiler pan or in a bowl sitting over a small pan of gently simmering water. Beat the egg yolks and sugar until thick.

3 Add the Marsala and beat with a wire whisk or a hand-held electric beater until the zabaglione is thick, light, and hot. Be patient—it will take 10–15 minutes to thicken.

4 Remove the zabaglione from the heat and cool a little, then fold gently into the chilled beaten cream with a metal spoon.

5 Divide the strawberries, reserving a few for decoration, between 6 tall glasses or serving bowls and spoon the creamy zabaglione over the top.

6 Chill in the refrigerator until needed. Alternatively, you can put them in the freezer for up to 1 hour. Just before serving, decorate the zabaglione with the reserved strawberries and some sprigs of fresh mint.

Serves 6

Baked Amaretto Peaches

Use unblemished, ripe peaches for this recipe. Stuffed peaches are popular in Italy, and you can experiment with savory fillings as well as sweet ones. Italian cheeses, such as Gorgonzola and Taleggio, as well as walnuts complement the luscious sweetness of the peaches. If wished, you can use nectarines instead.

4 large peaches
8 amaretti biscuits
1 egg yolk
1 tablespoon sugar
⅓ cup mascarpone cheese
1 tablespoon butter
4 tablespoons Amaretto liqueur

FOR THE AMARETTO CHEESE:
3 tablespoons fromage frais
3 tablespoons mascarpone cheese
1 tablespoon sugar
1 tablespoon Amaretto liqueur

1 Wash the peaches and pat dry with paper towels. Cut them in half and remove the pits. Carefully hollow out a little of the flesh to enlarge the cavity. Reserve the flesh you have removed for the filling.

2 Crush the amaretti biscuits with a rolling pin and mix well with the egg yolk, sugar, mascarpone cheese, and the reserved peach flesh.

3 Divide the mixture between the peaches and smooth the tops. Stand the stuffed peaches in a buttered baking dish. Dot them with butter, and sprinkle the Amaretto over the top.

4 Bake in a preheated oven at 325°F for about 20 minutes, until the amaretti filling is golden on top. Alternatively, you can place the peaches under a preheated hot broiler for about 5 minutes.

5 Meanwhile, make the Amaretto cheese. Beat the fromage frais into the mascarpone, and stir in the sugar and Amaretto liqueur. Serve with the warm peaches.

Serves 4

Opposite: Strawberry Zabaglione

Strawberry Almond **Shortcakes**

Eat these American shortcakes as a summer dessert or serve with homemade lemonade for afternoon tea. As a change from strawberries, try filling them with raspberries, cherries, or peaches instead.

2³/4 cups all-purpose flour
pinch of salt
3 teaspoons baking powder
1¹/4 sticks butter, softened
¹/4 cup sugar
⁵/8 cup heavy cream
melted butter, for brushing
powdered sugar, for dusting

FOR THE FILLING:
¹/2 cup mascarpone cheese
¹/2 cup low-fat fromage frais
1–2 tablespoons powdered sugar
1 pound strawberries
¹/4 cup toasted slivered almonds

1 Sift the flour, salt, and baking powder into a large mixing bowl. Rub in the butter until the mixture resembles bread crumbs. Stir in the sugar and the heavy cream. You should end up with a soft but not too sticky dough.

2 Turn out the dough on to a lightly floured surface and knead gently. Roll it out quite thickly—about ¹/2 inch thick. Cut into 2-inch rounds with a cookie cutter.

3 Arrange half of the shortcakes on a buttered cookie sheet and brush lightly with melted butter. Put the remaining shortcakes on top of the buttered ones.

4 Bake in a preheated oven at 450°F for about 10–15 minutes, until the shortcakes are well risen and golden brown. Remove from the oven and cool a little on a wire rack.

5 While the shortcakes are cooking, mix the mascarpone cheese and fromage frais in a bowl. Sweeten to taste with powdered sugar.

6 Split the cooked shortcakes in half while warm. Fill them with the strawberries, toasted slivered almonds, and mascarpone filling, and sandwich together. Dust lightly with powdered sugar and serve.

Serves 6

Peach and Blueberry **Crumble**

This is real comfort food—juicy fruit topped with a buttery, nutty crumble. The wonderful thing about crumbles is that they are so quick and easy to make. You can use almost any fruit; the usual choices are apples, pears, or rhubarb. However, this version combines tart blueberries with succulent peaches.

6 large peaches, skinned and pitted
2 cups blueberries
¹/3 cup sugar

FOR THE CRUMBLE:
1¹/2 cups all-purpose flour
¹/2 cup ground almonds
1¹/2 sticks butter, diced
¹/3 cup sugar
¹/4 cup slivered almonds or
chopped hazelnuts

1 Cut the peaches into quarters and place in a well buttered baking dish with the blueberries and sugar. Toss them gently together.

2 Make the crumble: put the flour and ground almonds in a bowl and rub in the butter gently with your fingertips until the mixture resembles fine bread crumbs.

3 Mix in the sugar and almonds or hazelnuts. Sprinkle with a tablespoon of water and stir well.

4 Spread the crumble over the fruit in the baking dish, leveling the top. Sprinkle a tablespoon of water over the top before baking. Bake the fruit crumble in a preheated hot oven at 400°F for 20 minutes, and then reduce the oven temperature to 350°F for a further 15 minutes, until the topping is crisp and golden.

4 Serve the crumble hot or warm with some vanilla ice cream, hot custard, whipped cream, or crème fraîche, according to choice.

Serves 6

Creole **Bananas** Flambé

Bananas are eaten throughout the Caribbean in both sweet and savory dishes. One of the easiest ways of cooking them is to grill or broil them and then serve with this wickedly rich toffee sauce.

4 ripe bananas, peeled
2 tablespoons brown sugar
juice of 1 lime
4 tablespoons dark rum

FOR THE CREAMY TOFFEE SAUCE:
1 1/4 cups heavy cream
1/4 cup soft brown sugar
2 teaspoons molasses

1 Put the bananas on a foil-lined broiler pan and sprinkle the sugar and lime juice over them. Put under a preheated hot broiler for a few minutes, turning until evenly golden.

2 Meanwhile, heat the cream, sugar, and molasses in a small pan, stirring to mix. Bring to a boil, and then remove from the heat.

3 Heat the rum and light it. Pour the flaming rum over the bananas and serve immediately with the creamy toffee sauce.

Serves 4

Filo Fruit **Parcels**

It is very important when making these little fruit pastries never to let the filo pastry dry out. Cover the paper-thin sheets you are going to use with some waxed paper and a damp cloth until you are ready for them. Virtually any fruit can be used: the soft berry fruits of summer, autumnal apples and pears mixed with blueberries or blackberries, or exotic tropical fruits, such as mango and papaya.

1 1/2 cups raspberries
1 tablespoon cassis (optional)
1/4 cup sugar
2 sheets filo pastry
2 tablespoons butter, melted
4 ounces soft goat's cheese
crème fraîche or thick cream, to serve

FOR THE FRUIT COULIS:
2 cups mixed raspberries and strawberries
1/4 cup sugar

1 Make the fruit coulis: put all the fruits and sugar in a large bowl and mix well. Set aside for at least 30 minutes. Put them into a blender or food processor and process until puréed. Push through a strainer to remove any seeds.

2 Put the raspberries in a bowl and pour over the cassis (if using). Leave to soak for 30 minutes, then mix in the sugar.

3 Cut one of the sheets of filo pastry in half lengthwise, then cut each piece of pastry into 3 squares, so that you have 6 in total.

4 Brush one filo square with melted butter and lay another square on top, brushing generously with some more melted butter. Then put a spoonful of the goat's cheese in the center and top with some raspberries.

5 Gather up the edges of the pastry and pull them together in the middle, twisting gently. Repeat with the remaining squares, and then do the same with the other sheet of filo pastry to make 3 more parcels.

6 Put the filo parcels on a buttered cookie sheet and bake in a preheated oven at 450°F for 8–10 minutes, until crisp and golden.

7 Serve the filo fruit parcels in a pool of fruit coulis with some crème fraîche or thick cream.

Serves 6

Provençal **Lavender** Ice Cream

1¼ cups light cream
2 sprigs of lavender
4 egg yolks
⁵/₈ cup vanilla sugar
1¼ cups heavy cream, whipped

TO SERVE:
¼ cup coarsely chopped
toasted almonds
few sprigs of lavender

This delicately flavored ice cream evokes memories of the lavender-scented hills of Provence. Make it in the summer when your lavender bushes are in bloom. You can easily make vanilla sugar by storing a vanilla bean in a jar of sugar.

1 Put the light cream and sprigs of lavender in a saucepan and heat through gently. Bring it just to a boil, remove from the heat and leave to infuse for 5 minutes.

2 Beat the egg yolks and vanilla sugar together in a bowl, until thick and creamy. Remove the lavender from the warm cream and beat the cream into the egg mixture.

3 Set the bowl over a small saucepan of simmering water and then stir constantly with a wooden spoon until the mixture thickens and coats the back of the spoon. Remove from the heat and set aside to cool.

4 Fold the whipped cream gently into the cooled custard and pour into a deep metal freezing container. Freeze on the lowest possible setting.

5 When the ice cream is partially frozen (the sides are frozen but the middle is still soft), remove from the freezer and stir well or beat with a hand whisk. Return to the freezer until it is frozen. Stir well or beat again with a hand whisk.

6 Serve the ice cream sprinkled with chopped toasted almonds and decorated with small sprigs of fresh lavender.

Serves 6

Variations

You can omit the lavender and add different flavorings to the basic vanilla ice cream.

1 Purée and strain uncooked summer fruits, such as strawberries, raspberries, or peaches, and stir into the cooked custard with the whipped cream.

2 After folding the whipped cream into the vanilla custard, fold in 4 ounces of shaved chocolate—use only the best-quality

bitter semisweet chocolate, which has a high cocoa solids content.

3 Use cinnamon sticks instead of lavender to infuse the cream, and add a teaspoon of ground cinnamon to the custard before freezing.

4 Cook and then purée and strain some apricots. Stir into the custard with some peach liqueur.

Orange Granita

An Italian granita differs from a sorbet in that it is more grainy in texture and comprised of frozen crystals. It is a very refreshing summer dessert. For this recipe, it is best to use the juice of freshly squeezed oranges rather than juice from a carton.

2 cups fresh orange juice
3–4 tablespoons sugar
sprigs of fresh mint, to decorate

1 Pour the orange juice and sugar into a blender or food processor and process briefly. Pour into a freezer container and then freeze the granita until half frozen.

2 Remove from the freezer and stir well to break up the ice crystals. Return to the freezer for 30 minutes, then remove and stir again.

3 Repeat this stirring process every 30 minutes over the next 3–4 hours, then remove from the freezer and serve in tall glasses.

Serves 6–8

Caribbean **Sorbet**

If wished, you can add a little white rum to the sorbet mixture before freezing. If guavas are not available, use mangoes or papayas instead.

2–3 ripe guavas, peeled and sliced
⁵/₈ cup sugar
2 cups water
5 ripe bananas, peeled and sliced
juice of 2 limes
chocolate sauce, to serve (see below)

1 Put the guavas, sugar, and water in a saucepan and simmer gently over low heat, until the fruit is tender. Add the bananas and simmer for about 5 minutes, until softened.

2 Allow to cool a little, then strain to remove the seeds. When completely cold, stir in the lime juice.

3 Pour the strained fruit mixture into a freezer container and freeze until half-frozen. Remove from the freezer and stir well or beat with a hand whisk. Replace in the freezer until the sorbet is frozen.

4 Serve the sorbet in scoops in a pool of cold chocolate sauce.

Serves 6

Christmas Sorbet

Serve this fresh, citrusy sorbet at Christmas, especially after rich and heavy meals. It tastes particularly good with chocolate sauce.

1¹/₄ cups sugar
2¹/₂ cups water
6 cloves
9 large satsumas, tangerines, or clementines

FOR THE CHOCOLATE SAUCE:
8 ounces bitter semisweet chocolate
¹/₂ cup heavy cream
¹/₂ cup milk
2 tablespoons sugar

1 Put the sugar, water, and cloves in a saucepan. Heat gently, stirring all the time, until the sugar dissolves and the liquid is clear.

2 Bring to a boil, and boil for 2–3 minutes, until the syrup thickens. Let stand until the syrup is cold, then remove the cloves.

3 Squeeze the juice from 8 satsumas or tangerines and stir into the cold sugar syrup. Pour into a freezing container and freeze for 2–3 hours, until half-frozen. Then remove from the freezer and beat with a hand whisk. Replace in the freezer until the sorbet has frozen solid.

4 Meanwhile, make the chocolate sauce. Break the chocolate into pieces and place them in a bowl over a saucepan of gently simmering water, until the chocolate melts. Remove from the heat.

5 Put the heavy cream, milk, and sugar in a saucepan and bring to the boil, stirring all the time. Stir into the melted chocolate and then leave the chocolate sauce to cool.

6 Serve the frozen sorbet in scoops in a pool of cold chocolate sauce, decorated with peeled sections from the remaining satsuma or tangerine.

Serves 6

Baking

In the kitchen, there is nothing more wonderful than the aroma of freshly baked

bread and cakes. Home baking can play an important role in today's contemporary,

healthy vegetarian diet, and there are lots of recipes for delicious and unusual breads,

scones, and cakes in this chapter. Baking is very enjoyable and

therapeutic as well as being surprisingly easy.

Basic White **Bread**

12 cups all-purpose white
flour
4 teaspoons salt
2 tablespoons vegetable margarine
2 teaspoons sugar
2 envelopes easy-blend yeast
1 cup milk
2¼ cups water
milk or beaten egg, for glazing

FOR THE ITALIAN
GARLIC BREAD:
3 tablespoons sun-dried tomatoes
in oil, chopped
2 garlic cloves, minced
½ cup black olives, pitted
and chopped
3 tablespoons tomato paste

FOR THE CHEESE AND
HERB BREAD:
½ cup grated cheese
1 teaspoon dried thyme
1 small red chili, seeded
and chopped

This basic bread recipe can be flavored in many ways, and two delicious variations are given below. If wished, you can make rolls instead of loaves, in which case you should shorten the baking time to 18–20 minutes.

1 Sift the white flour and salt into a large mixing bowl. Cut the margarine into small pieces and rub into the flour. Stir in the sugar and easy-blend yeast. Heat the milk and water until hand-hot, then mix into the flour to form a soft dough.

2 Turn out on to a lightly floured surface and knead well for 5–10 minutes, until the dough is elastic and smooth. Put the dough in a lightly oiled bowl, cover, and leave in a warm place for about 1 hour, until risen and doubled in size.

3 Punch the dough down with your fists and divide into 3 pieces. Shape one piece of dough into a loaf and place in a greased loaf pan. Cover with a cloth and leave in a warm place to rise to the top of the pan.

4 Roll out the second piece of dough. Mix all the Italian garlic filling ingredients together and spread over the dough. Roll up and pat into a loaf. Place in a greased loaf pan. Cover and leave in a warm place.

5 Roll out the remaining dough and sprinkle with the cheese and herb filling. Roll up and place in a greased loaf pan or shape into rolls. Cover and leave in a warm place.

6 When the dough rises to the top of the pans, brush lightly with a little milk or beaten egg and bake in a preheated hot oven at 425°F for about 30 minutes. When the loaves are ready, they will sound hollow when you tap the bottoms. Cool on a wire rack.

Makes 3 loaves

Basic White Bread

Italian **Focaccia**

This flat bread can be made into small loaves or rolls, topped with fruity olive oil. You can also experiment with different toppings.

FOR THE DOUGH:
4¹/₂ cups white flour
¹/₂ teaspoon salt
1 teaspoon brown sugar
3 teaspoons easy-blend yeast
1¹/₄ cups warm water
2 tablespoons olive oil

1 Sift the flour and salt into a large mixing bowl. Stir in the brown sugar and yeast, and then make a hollow in the center of the flour.

2 Pour in the warm water and olive oil and mix well to form a soft dough. Turn out on to a lightly floured surface and knead for 10 minutes, until the dough is silky and elastic.

3 Put the dough in an oiled bowl, cover with plastic wrap or a clean cloth, and leave in a warm place until risen and doubled in size.

4 Turn out the dough and punch it down. Knead lightly, then either roll the dough out to a large oval or a rectangle, or cut into 4 pieces and roll out each one individually. Prick the dough all over with a fork and place on an oiled cookie sheet.

5 Add the topping of your choice and bake in a preheated hot oven at 425°F: 20 minutes for a large loaf; or 15 minutes for smaller ones. Do not allow the toppings to brown or burn. Cover with some kitchen foil or reduce the oven temperature to 375°F if necessary. The cooked focaccia should look crisp and golden. Cool on a wire rack.

Makes 1 large loaf or 4 small ones

Olive and garlic topping

²/₃ cup mixed black and green olives
3–4 garlic cloves, peeled and thinly sliced
10–12 fresh basil leaves
1 teaspoon coarse sea salt crystals
2 tablespoons olive oil

Press the olives and slivers of garlic lightly into the dough. Tear each basil leaf into 2 or 3 pieces and push them into the dough. Sprinkle with sea salt and pour a little olive oil over the top.

Sun-dried tomato topping

2 tablespoons sun-dried tomatoes in oil, chopped
1 tablespoon coarsely chopped fresh sage
freshly ground mixed peppercorns (green, black, red)
2 tablespoons olive oil

Scatter the sun-dried tomatoes over the dough and press them in lightly. Sprinkle with sage and the freshly ground peppercorns, then drizzle the olive oil over the top.

Rosemary topping

2 tablespoons fresh rosemary leaves
1 teaspoon coarse sea salt crystals
2 tablespoons olive oil

Scatter the rosemary and sea salt over the dough, then sprinkle the oil over the top.

Provençal **Olive** Bread

For a really authentic flavor, try to obtain some small black or purple Niçoise olives. Otherwise, use oil-cured Italian, Greek, or Spanish olives.

6³/₄ cups white bread flour
2 teaspoons salt
1 envelope easy-blend yeast
2 cups warm water
4 tablespoons olive oil
1 cup black olives, pitted
and coarsely chopped

1 Sift the flour and salt into a large mixing bowl, mix in the yeast and make a hollow in the center.

2 Pour in the warm water and olive oil and mix well with your hand, drawing in the flour from the sides of the bowl. You should end up with a soft ball of dough that leaves the sides of the bowl clean.

3 Knead the dough for about 10 minutes on a lightly floured surface, until it is silky and elastic. Place in an oiled bowl, cover with some plastic wrap or a clean cloth, and leave in a warm place until the dough has risen and doubled in size.

4 Punch down the dough to remove the air bubbles. Press it out with your hands and sprinkle with the black olives. Fold the dough over the olives and knead well to distribute them evenly throughout.

5 Cut the dough in half and shape each piece into a round loaf. Place the loaves on an oiled cookie sheet, cover with a clean cloth, and leave in a warm place for about 30 minutes, until doubled in size.

6 Bake the loaves in a preheated hot oven at 425°F for 25–30 minutes. If the loaves are browning too quickly, then lower the oven temperature to 400°F after 15 minutes. Remove the cooked loaves from the oven and cool on a wire rack.

Makes 2 loaves

Thyme, Onion, and Garlic **Bread**

This fragrant bread, flavored with garlic and herbs, is the perfect partner to cheese, olives, and little Mediterranean gherkins.

3¹/₄ cups whole-wheat flour
¹/₂ teaspoon salt
2 teaspoons fresh thyme leaves
1 small onion, finely chopped
2 garlic cloves, minced
¹/₂ envelope easy-blend yeast
1 cup warm
milk and water
2 tablespoons olive oil
1 egg, beaten

1 Sift the flour and salt into a mixing bowl and stir in the thyme, onion, garlic, and easy-blend yeast. Make a hollow in the center and pour in the warm milk and water, olive oil, and beaten egg. Mix to form a ball of soft dough which leaves the sides of the bowl clean.

2 Turn the dough out on to a lightly floured board and knead for about 10 minutes, until the dough is really elastic. Place in an oiled bowl, cover, and leave in a warm place until risen and doubled in size.

3 Punch the dough down to get rid of any air bubbles. Knead lightly and shape into a loaf. Place in a greased 1-pound loaf pan, cover with a clean cloth and leave to rise to the top of the pan in a warm place.

4 Bake the loaf in a preheated hot oven at 450°F for about 30 minutes. Remove the loaf from the pan and cool on a wire rack.

Makes 1 loaf

Variations

1 Make the dough, omitting the thyme, onion, and garlic. After rising and punching back, mix 1 tablespoon crushed red and green peppercorns into the dough.

2 Add some mixed sunflower, pumpkin, and poppy seeds to the flour and yeast mixture before adding the warm liquid.

Granary loaves

Serves 6

These moist, nutty loaves stay fresh for several days, and can be frozen successfully. You can bake a large batch and freeze any loaves you do not want to eat immediately. If wished, you can use two envelopes of easy-blend yeast rather than fresh yeast. Of course, you can simplify the process and make the bread in a food processor or food mixer if you have a special dough attachment or a dough hook.

13 cups whole-wheat flour
4 teaspoons salt
2 tablespoons vegetable
margarine, diced
²/₃ cup cracked wheat
2 tablespoons wheat germ
¼ cup bran
2 tablespoons brown sugar
2 tablespoons molasses
3³/₄ cups warm water
1¹/₂ ounces fresh yeast
beaten egg or milk, to glaze
cracked wheat, for decoration

1 Sift the flour and salt into a large mixing bowl, and then rub in the margarine until thoroughly blended. Next, stir in the cracked wheat, wheat germ, bran, and brown sugar.

2 Stir the molasses into the warm water and add 2 tablespoons of the mixture to the fresh yeast. Stir well to mix. Make a hollow in the center of the flour mixture and pour in the yeast and warm water. Mix well to form a smooth dough that leaves the sides of the bowl clean.

3 Turn the dough out on to a lightly floured surface and knead for 10

minutes, until it is really smooth, silky, and elastic. When kneading, always fold the dough inward toward you with one hand while pushing it away from you with the other hand. Give the dough a quarter-turn and repeat. Place the dough in an oiled bowl, cover with some plastic wrap or a clean cloth, and leave in a warm place until it has risen and doubled in size.

4 Punch the dough down with your fists to knock out any air bubbles, and knead lightly. Cut into 3 pieces and shape into loaves. Place them on a well greased cookie sheet, cover with a clean cloth, and leave in a warm place until doubled in size. Alternatively, you can shape the dough into loaves and place each one in a well greased 1-pound loaf pan, and leave in a warm place until the dough rises to the top of the pans. Or you can make braided loaves or rolls. Glaze the loaves with beaten egg or milk, and sprinkle with cracked wheat. Bake in a preheated hot oven at 450°F for 30–35 minutes. If the bases sound hollow when tapped with your knuckles, then the loaves are cooked. Remove from the pans or tray and cool on a wire rack.

Baileys Cheese Scones

These delicious cheese scones are the speciality of Baileys Tearooms in Bury St. Edmunds, England, and are best served warm and buttered.

4¹/2 cups self-rising flour
2 level teaspoons baking powder
1 stick butter, softened
2 cups grated Cheddar cheese
2 heaped teaspoons
whole grain mustard
¹/2 cup milk, to mix
2 teaspoons sesame seeds

1 Sift the flour and baking powder into a mixing bowl, and rub in the butter with your fingertips. Stir in the grated cheese and mustard.

2 Add sufficient milk to form a workable soft dough, and then turn out on to a lightly floured surface.

3 Lightly roll out the dough, about 1¹/2 inches thick. Cut into rounds with a 2-inch cookie cutter, and place on a cookie sheet. Let stand for 10 minutes, then brush the tops with milk and sprinkle with sesame seeds.

4 Bake the scones near the top of a preheated oven at 400°F for 12–15 minutes, until risen and golden brown. Cool slightly on a wire rack before serving.

Makes 20 scones

Carrot and Herb Muffins

These savory little muffins are flavored with cheese, carrot, onion, and fresh herbs. They are ideal for brunches and picnics. If wished, you can split and butter them.

2¹/4 cups whole-wheat
self-rising flour
pinch of salt
1 teaspoon baking powder
4 tablespoons butter, softened
1 cup grated Swiss or
Cheddar cheese
1 carrot, grated
1 onion, grated
small bunch chopped chives
1 egg, beaten
¹/2 cup milk

1 Sift the flour, salt, and baking powder into a mixing bowl, and rub in the butter with your fingertips. Mix in three-quarters of the grated cheese, with the carrot and onion, then stir in the chives.

2 Stir in the beaten egg and milk to bind the muffin batter. Divide between 8 buttered deep muffin pans,

then sprinkle the tops lightly with the remaining grated cheese.

3 Bake in a preheated oven at 400°F for about 15 minutes, until the muffins rise and are golden. Cool the muffins slightly on a wire rack before serving.

Makes 8 muffins

Old-fashioned Shortbread

This Scottish shortbread is made with healthy whole-wheat flour.

1 stick butter, diced
1¹/4 cups whole-wheat flour
¹/4 cup rice flour or semolina
¹/4 cup soft brown sugar
sugar, for dredging

1 Rub the butter into the whole-wheat and rice flours, and stir in the brown sugar. Mix to a dough, then knead on a lightly floured board.

2 Roll out the dough to a large round, ¹/4 inch thick, and place on a cookie sheet. Prick all over with a fork.

3 Bake in a preheated oven at 350°F for 20–25 minutes. Cut into triangles while the shortbread is warm and leave on the cookie sheet to cool. Dredge with sugar before serving.

Makes 12 triangles

Apricot Slices

Afternoon coffee or tea is one of life's great pleasures. These apricot slices are perfect on a cold winter's afternoon in front of a blazing fire.

2/3 cup dried apricots
1 cup whole-wheat flour
pinch of salt
1 cup old-fashioned oats
2 tablespoons wheat germ
1 1/4 sticks butter, softened
2/3 cup soft brown sugar
1/4 cup dried coconut
1 teaspoon baking soda
2 teaspoons boiling water

1 Put the apricots in a bowl, cover with water, and leave to soak for about 2 hours. Transfer to a small saucepan and simmer gently over low heat for about 10 minutes, or until softened but still firm. Drain the apricots and set aside.

2 Put the flour, salt, oats, and wheat germ in a mixing bowl. Rub in the butter, then stir in the sugar and coconut. Dissolve the baking soda in the boiling water and stir into the crumble mixture.

3 Press half of the crumble mixture into a buttered 8-inch square shallow baking pan. Press down well to cover the base and then level it. Then spread the drained, cooked apricots evenly over the top. Cover with the remaining crumble mixture and press down firmly, smoothing out the surface.

4 Bake in a preheated oven at 350°F for 30–35 minutes, until the crumble topping is cooked and golden brown. Cool in the pan and then cut into 12 slices.

Makes 12 slices

Banana Bread

This is served for breakfast throughout the Caribbean archipelago of islands. However, you can serve it sliced and buttered for afternoon tea.

1 stick butter, softened
3/4 cup sugar
2 eggs
3 large ripe bananas, peeled and mashed
2/3 cup coarsely chopped pecans
2 1/4 cups self-rising flour
1/2 teaspoon salt
1/2 teaspoon nutmeg
good pinch of cinnamon
few drops of vanilla extract
1/2 teaspoon baking soda

1 Beat the butter and sugar in a mixing bowl. Beat in the eggs, one at a time. Stir in the mashed bananas and pecans, then sift the flour, salt, and spices into the batter. Fold in gently, then stir in the vanilla extract and baking soda.

2 Line a buttered 1-pound loaf pan with parchment paper, and spoon the banana batter into the pan. Level the top, and then bake in a preheated oven at 350°F for about 1 hour. Test whether the banana bread is cooked by inserting a metal skewer into the center of the loaf. It is ready when the skewer comes out clean.

3 Allow the banana bread to cool in the pan for 10 minutes, and then turn out the loaf on to a wire rack. When it is completely cold, cut into slices to serve. The banana bread keeps well, wrapped in kitchen foil, for several days. It also freezes successfully.

Makes 1 loaf

Date and **Walnut** Loaf

This is a really old-fashioned loaf to serve at afternoon tea. Wrap it up in foil and it will stay moist and delicious for several days.

1 cup water
³/₄ cup soft brown sugar
2 tablespoons butter
1 teaspoon baking soda
³/₄ cup chopped dates
2 eggs, beaten
2¹/₄ cups all-purpose or
whole-wheat flour
³/₄ cup chopped walnuts

1 Bring the water to the boil in a saucepan, then add the sugar, butter, baking soda, and dates. Reduce the heat and stir gently over low heat until the sugar dissolves.

2 Remove the pan from the heat, allow to cool a little and then stir in the beaten eggs. Mix thoroughly and then add the flour and chopped walnuts.

3 Butter a 1-pound loaf pan and then line it with parchment paper. Pour the date and walnut batter into the lined pan and bake in a preheated oven at 375°F for 25–30 minutes, until the loaf rises and is golden brown.

4 Leave the loaf in the pan for about 10 minutes, and then turn out on to a wire rack to cool. When cold, serve sliced and buttered.

Makes 1 loaf

Zucchini Nut Loaf

3 eggs
³/₄ cup soft brown sugar
¹/₂ cup corn
or walnut oil
1¹/₄ cups whole-wheat flour
1¹/₄ cups all-purpose flour
1 heaped teaspoon baking powder
¹/₂ teaspoon baking soda
1 teaspoon cinnamon
¹/₂ teaspoon allspice
¹/₂ teaspoon ground ginger
pinch of salt
2 medium zucchini, finely grated
¹/₃ cup chopped dates
¹/₃ cup chopped hazelnuts or
walnuts

Here's an unusual spicy loaf with a difference. Made with oil instead of butter and flecked with grated green zucchini, it is delicious served sliced and buttered for afternoon tea.

1 Beat the eggs, sugar, and oil in a mixing bowl or food processor until well blended. Gently fold in the sifted flours, baking powder, baking soda, spices, and salt. Fold in the grated zucchini (having squeezed out any moisture), dates, and chopped hazelnuts or walnuts.

2 Butter a 1-pound loaf pan and line with parchment paper. Pour in the mixture and level the top. Bake in a preheated oven at 350°F for 1¹/₄ hours, or until it rises and is golden.

To test whether the loaf is cooked, insert a skewer in the center—it should come out clean.

3 Cool in the pan for 10–15 minutes, then turn out on to a wire rack. Serve sliced and buttered.

Makes 1 loaf

Opposite: Date and Walnut Loaf (in the foreground) and Zucchini Nut Loaf

Sticky **Ginger** Cake

1 stick butter, softened

1/2 cup soft brown sugar

2 large eggs

2 1/4 cups all-purpose flour

1 teaspoon baking powder

2 teaspoons ground ginger

1 teaspoon ground allspice

1 cup molasses

4 ounces stem ginger in syrup, coarsely chopped

1 teaspoon baking soda

3 tablespoons warm milk

FOR THE FROSTING:

juice of 1/2 lemon

1/2 cup powdered sugar, sifted

stem ginger pieces, for decoration

Impossibly dark, wickedly sticky and unbelievably moist, this has to be the best ginger cake ever. It will keep for at least a week stored in an airtight container; indeed, it improves after a couple of days if you can bear to forgo eating it immediately.

1 Cream the butter and sugar in a bowl or a food processor. Beat in the eggs, one at a time, and then sift in the flour, baking powder, and spices. Fold gently into the batter.

2 Stir in the molasses and stem ginger. Blend the baking soda with the warm milk, and stir gently into the cake batter. If the batter is a bit too thick, you can thin it down with some more milk or a little more syrup from the stem ginger jar.

3 Butter and line a 7-inch round cake pan, and pour in the cake mixture. Bake in a preheated oven at 325°F for 1 1/4 hours, then lower the oven temperature to 300°F for a further 30 minutes.

4 Allow the cake to cool in the pan and then turn it out. Don't worry if it sinks a little in the middle—just turn the cake over and prepare to decorate the base instead of the top.

5 Mix the lemon juice and powdered sugar to a smooth paste and spoon over the top of the cake so that the frosting drizzles down the sides. Decorate the cake with pieces of stem ginger.

Makes 1 cake

American Cranberry **Muffins**

1/2 cup dried cranberries

1 cup milk or buttermilk

2 1/4 cups all-purpose flour

1 1/2 teaspoons baking powder

1/2 teaspoon salt

1/4 cup sugar

1 large egg, beaten

grated rind of 1 orange

4 tablespoons butter, melted

FOR THE TOPPING:

1/4 cup chopped walnuts

3 tablespoons crushed sugar crystals

These muffins are quick and easy to make. Serve them warm and fresh from the oven for breakfast or brunch. If wished, you can substitute dried blueberries for the cranberries.

1 Put the dried cranberries in a bowl and add the milk or buttermilk. Set aside to soak for 10–15 minutes.

2 Sift the flour and baking powder into a mixing bowl. Add the salt and sugar and stir well. Make a hollow in the center of the flour.

3 Mix the beaten egg, orange rind, and melted butter into the milk and cranberries. Pour into the hollow in the flour, and mix gently together.

4 Divide the muffin batter between 12 well-buttered muffin pans. Sprinkle the tops with the chopped walnuts and sugar crystals.

5 Bake in a preheated oven at 400°F for 20 minutes, until the muffins rise and are golden. Cool for 10–15 minutes, then serve warm.

Makes 12 muffins

Opposite: Cranberry Muffins

Basic Recipes

In the following pages you will find some useful basic recipes for sauces, dressings, salsas, pie crust, and croutons. Many of these are referred to throughout this book, especially the classic vegetable broth, which forms the basis of many soups and stews. The flavor is so superior to commercial bouillon cubes that it is well worth making in bulk and freezing until required.

Creamy **Mushroom** Sauce

3/4 pound mushrooms (white, morels, chanterelles, ceps, etc.)
6 tablespoons butter
5 tablespoons Marsala
1/4 cup vegetable broth
1/2 cup half and half
freshly ground black pepper

Serve this sauce with Layered Nut Roast (see page 74) or with any cooked pasta.

1 Slice the mushrooms thinly. Fry them in the butter in a large skillet until golden brown.

2 Add the Marsala and vegetable broth and bring to a boil. Let the sauce simmer until it reduces and starts to turn syrupy.

3 Stir in the half and half and simmer gently for a few minutes. Season to taste with black pepper.

Makes 1 cup

Garlic Croutons

Serve these with vegetable soups or sprinkled over crisp green salads.

1 Cut the crusts off the bread and cut it into small cubes. Put them in a bowl with the olive oil and garlic and toss gently together.

2 Arrange the croutons on a cookie sheet and bake in a preheated oven

4 thick slices crusty white bread
2 tablespoons fruity green olive oil
2 garlic cloves, minced

at 350°F for 8–10 minutes, until the croutons are crisp and golden. Check them from time to time to make sure

Variation

For herb croutons, substitute 1–2 tablespoons finely chopped fresh herbs for the garlic cloves, and proceed as described.

that they do not become too brown. Remove and cool.

Fresh **Avocado** Sauce

1 large ripe avocado
2 tablespoons mayonnaise
1 cup low-fat fromage frais
dash of lemon juice

Serve this quick and easy sauce with vegetable burgers, or pile into split pita breads with salad.

Peel the avocado, remove the pit, and mash the flesh. Mix in the mayonnaise and fromage frais, and add lemon juice to taste. This sauce should be made just before eating, or the avocado will discolor.

Makes 1 cup

Creamy **Mayonnaise**

To make a perfect mayonnaise all the ingredients should be at room temperature. Add the oil very slowly—drop by drop, and then in a thin stream—or the mayonnaise may curdle. If the worst happens and it does curdle, don't panic. Just break another egg yolk into a clean bowl and then slowly beat in the curdled mayonnaise.

2 egg yolks
good pinch of salt
1 tablespoon white wine vinegar
1 teaspoon powdered mustard
freshly ground black pepper
1 1/4 cups olive oil
squeeze of lemon juice

1 Beat the egg yolks, salt, wine vinegar, mustard, and black pepper together in a large bowl, until well blended. Use a wire whisk or an electric hand-held one.

2 Start adding the olive oil, drop by drop, beating all the time. When the sauce starts to thicken, add the remaining oil in a thin stream, still beating all the time.

3 Stir in a tablespoon of boiling water and a squeeze of lemon juice. Store the mayonnaise in a covered container in the refrigerator.

Makes 1 1/4 cups

> ### **Variations**
> ....
> *You can flavor the basic mayonnaise with chopped fresh herbs (chives, dill, tarragon), minced garlic cloves or chopped capers.*

Vegetable **Broth**

3 3/4 cups water
2 onions, peeled and sliced
2 carrots, peeled and halved
1 leek, cleaned, trimmed, and halved
2 celery stalks, halved
1 bay leaf
few parsley stalks
few sprigs of thyme
few celery leaves
10 black peppercorns
good pinch of salt

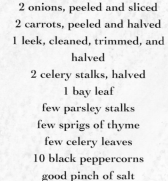

Use this broth for making stews and soups, and in any recipes that call for broth. It has a stronger, better flavor than broths made with bouillon cubes. If wished, you can double the quantities given here, and freeze some broth for the future.

1 Put the water, vegetables, herbs, and seasonings in a large saucepan.

2 Bring to a boil, then cover the pan and simmer very gently for 1 1/2 hours. Strain and use.

Makes 2 1/2 cups

Barbecue **Sauce**

Serve this tangy sauce with grilled vegetables and kebabs.

1 onion, finely chopped
2 garlic cloves, minced
2 tablespoons olive oil
1¹/₂ cups canned chopped tomatoes
1 tablespoon white wine vinegar
1 tablespoon soft brown sugar
¹/₂ teaspoon cayenne pepper

1 teaspoon Dijon mustard
1 thick slice of lemon
2 tablespoons Worcestershire sauce
3 tablespoons tomato ketchup
1 tablespoon tomato paste
salt and freshly ground black pepper

1 Fry the onion and garlic gently in the oil until soft and golden. Add the canned tomatoes, vinegar, sugar, cayenne, mustard and lemon. Bring to a boil, then reduce the heat a little and cook vigorously for about 15 minutes, until the sauce thickens.

2 Add the remaining ingredients and continue cooking for another 5 minutes, or until thick. Remove the slice of lemon just before serving.

Makes 1¹/₄ cups

Exotic Fruit **Salsa**

1 ripe mango, peeled, pitted, and diced
1 papaya, peeled, seeded, and diced
1 pound ripe tomatoes, skinned, seeded, and chopped
1 small red onion, finely chopped
1 red bell pepper, seeded and diced
2 hot red chilies, seeded and finely chopped
1 tablespoon olive oil
juice of 1 lime
salt and freshly ground black pepper
3 tablespoons chopped cilantro leaves

You can serve this salsa with spicy Mexican and Indian dishes, grilled and barbecued vegetables, or simply with bread and cheese.

Mix the mango, papaya, tomatoes, onion, red bell pepper, and chilies in a bowl. Add the olive oil and lime juice and toss together. Season to taste with salt and pepper, and stir in the cilantro leaves.

Serves 4

Blue Cheese Pasta Sauce

You can use any blue cheese (Gorgonzola, Roquefort, etc.) in this rich, creamy sauce for pasta. For a quick meal, simply toss some tagliatelle, pappardelle, or fettuccine in the sauce and serve with a crisp green salad.

2 cups heavy cream
4 tablespoons butter, diced
4 ounces blue cheese, cubed
salt and freshly ground black pepper

Pour the cream into a saucepan and heat through gently until it starts bubbling. Add the butter, reduce the heat, and simmer gently for 10 minutes, until reduced and creamy. Stir in the blue cheese, season with salt and pepper, and toss with the pasta of your choice.

Serves 4

Classic **Vinaigrette** Dressing

This dressing will add interest to any green, mixed, tomato, or potato salad. You can vary it in many ways as outlined below. The only hard and fast rule is that you must use good quality olive oil.

3 tablespoons extra-virgin olive oil
1 tablespoon white wine vinegar
1 teaspoon Dijon mustard
pinch of sugar

Measure the olive oil and wine vinegar into a small bowl and blend together. Stir in the mustard and sugar, until thoroughly blended.

Makes ¹/₄ cup dressing

Variations

1 *Substitute red wine vinegar, tarragon vinegar, cider vinegar, balsamic vinegar, lemon, or lime juice for the white wine vinegar.*

2 *Add a minced garlic clove and/or some finely chopped fresh herbs, especially chives and tarragon.*

Guacamole

2 ripe avocados
juice of 1 small lime
2 garlic cloves, minced
4 scallions, finely chopped
1 hot green chili, seeded and chopped
2 ripe tomatoes, skinned and finely chopped
2 tablespoons chopped fresh cilantro
salt and freshly ground black pepper

Serve this spicy green sauce with Mexican dishes, as a dip with raw vegetables or tortilla chips, or mixed with olive oil and wine vinegar as a salad dresing. Add more chilies if you like really hot food.

Cut the avocados in half, and then remove the peel and pits. Scoop out the flesh. Put the avocado in a bowl with the lime juice, and mash coarsely. Stir in the garlic, scallions, chili, tomatoes, and cilantro to make a thick sauce. Season to taste with salt and plenty of freshly ground black pepper. Cover the bowl and refrigerate until required. The lime juice will help prevent the avocado discoloring, but the guacamole should be eaten within a few hours of making if you want it to look really fresh and a delicate creamy green color.

Serves 4–6

Pie Crust

Use this pie crust for making sweet and savory tarts and pies. If wished, you can flavor it with some grated cheese, chopped herbs, mustard, grated orange and lemon rind, or ground nuts.

2¹/₄ cups all-purpose flour
pinch of salt
1 stick butter or margarine, at room temperature
3–4 tablespoons cold water, to mix

Sift the flour and salt into a large bowl. Cut the butter or margarine into small pieces and rub into the flour with your fingertips until the mixture resembles fine bread crumbs. Mix in the cold water with a round-bladed knife, until the mixture binds to form a soft, smooth dough that leaves the sides of the bowl clean. Wrap the dough in some kitchen foil or a plastic bag and leave to rest in the refrigerator for 30 minutes before rolling out.

Makes 8 ounces pie crust

Index

North American Vegetarian Society

The North American Vegetarian Society promotes the health, nutritional, environmental, and compassionate benefits of a meatless diet. It also

■ Organizes the annual Vegetarian Summerfest conference.

■ Promotes World Vegetarian Day (October 1) and Vegetarian Awareness Month (October).

■ Publishes *Vegetarian Voice*, a quarterly magazine with articles on essential health, nutrition, animal rights, environmental, vegetarian, and consumer issues.

■ Offers a free 16-page booklet with recipes, "Vegetarianism: Answers to the Most Commonly Asked Questions." A booklet on vegetarian nutrition, "Good Nutrition: A Look at Vegetarian Basics," and a booklet on the environment, "Vegetarianism: Tipping the Scales for the Environment." To obtain, send a self-addressed stamped envelope to NAVS, Box 72Q, Dolgeville, NY 13329. (518) 568-7970 or email at navs@telenet.net.

Membership Information

Regular members are vegetarians—fully and consistently abstaining from flesh, fish, and fowl. Associate members are nonvegetarians. As a member, you will receive an annual subscription to *Vegetarian Voice*. Members are also entitled a ten percent discount on all book and merchandise offers as well as reduced registration at the annual Vegetarian Summerfest conference.

Please send inquiries to NAVS, Box 72, Dolgeville, NY 13329, call (518) 568-7970, or email navs@telenet.net.